The
Five Life
Decisions

The
Five Life
Decisions

How Economic
Principles
and 18 Million
Millennials Can
Guide Your
Thinking

Robert T. Michael

THE UNIVERSITY OF CHICAGO PRESS

CHICAGO AND LONDON

Robert T. Michael is the founding dean and Eliakim Hastings Moore Distinguished Service Professor Emeritus of the Harris School of Public Policy Studies at the University of Chicago. He is also a senior fellow at the National Opinion Research Center at the University of Chicago.

The University of Chicago Press, Chicago 60637
The University of Chicago Press, Ltd., London
© 2016 by Robert T. Michael
All rights reserved. Published 2016.
Printed in the United States of America

25 24 23 22 21 20 19 18 17 16   1 2 3 4 5

ISBN-13: 978-0-226-35444-6 (paper)
ISBN-13: 978-0-226-35458-3 (e-book)
DOI: 10.7208/chicago/9780226354583.001.0001

Library of Congress Cataloging-in-Publication Data

Names: Michael, Robert T., author.
Title: The five life decisions: how economic principles and 18 milion millennials can guide your thinking / Robert T. Michael.
Description: Chicago; London: The University of Chicago Press, 2016. | Includes bibliographical references and index.
Identifiers: LCCN 2015039592 | ISBN 9780226354446 (pbk.: alk. paper) | ISBN 978022635483 (e-book)
Subjects: LCSH: Young adults—United States. | Choice (Psychology)—Social aspects. | Choice (Psychology)—Economic aspects. | Decision making. | Decision making—Social aspects. | Decision making—Economic aspects. | Rational choice theory. | Young adults—United States—Social conditions—21st century.
Classification: LCC HQ799.7 .M53 2016 | DDC 305.242—dc23 LC record available at http://lccn.loc.gov/2015039592

♾ This paper meets the requirements of ANSI/NISO Z39.48-1992 (Permanence of Paper).

To my grandchildren
Daniel Olson, Sadie Olson, Zachary Michael, and Kara Michael

Contents

Acknowledgments

An author needs a lot of advice from friends and patience from family when writing a book. I've benefited from both, thankfully. Early on, my colleagues Dan Black, Tom Coleman, and Allen Sanderson were helpful in sharing with me their thoughts about the big concepts and ideas most useful in making life decisions. Charlie Wheelan and Helen Roberts encouraged me and gave me good guidance that I greatly appreciate.

Carolina Milesi worked with me to construct the NLSY97 data files used in the book. The files were created for another reason but were of great convenience in this project, which I have undertaken alone. Any calculation errors in the tables here are my responsibility.

With a first draft in hand, several college students read the whole manuscript and gave me reactions from a perspective that was vital to communicating with twenty-something men and women. I thank Sarah Claypoole, Alec Goodwin, Karin Gorski, Sara Beth Hoffman, Hana Khosla, Emily Modlin, Sarah Olson, and Samantha Weiss for that help.

At a later stage, my young colleagues NaYoung Rim and Pallavi Vyas read through the manuscript with care and helped me get some of the arguments in better balance. My good friend Ellen Cohen read through the draft as well and offered valuable comments and a lot of encouragement. My partner, Kennette Benedict, not only showed a lot of patience with me during many days at the desk, but also encouraged me in this project from beginning to end and offered sage guidance along the way.

My editor, Joe Jackson, more than earned his stripes as an editor, reading every sentence at least once and encouraged me to push back time and time again. His careful editing has dramatically improved the book. I am much in his debt.

ONE | Making Choices

We all make choices in life. The hard thing is to live with them.

THE WORDS (2012)

From the time you get up in the morning, you begin to make choices—about what to eat for breakfast, what to wear, and on and on. A lot of these decisions are pretty trivial. But now and then, one of them is really important, and it can impact you throughout your life.

This is a book about five big decisions that you'll face. Three of these choices have a lot to do with how and with whom you spend much of your adult life. The other two help define your capabilities, so they have a profound effect on the other three. While these are not the only big decisions you'll face, we'll focus on them because they have lifetime consequences for you and because they are interconnected. As we discuss these five, you'll see that a lot of what we consider can be useful to you in making other decisions as well.

Now, this isn't a book that tells you what to choose for any of these five life decisions. Sorry. It might, at first, seem nice if someone came along and told you what to do, how to do it, when to do it, and so forth, and relieved you of having to make choices. But when you think about it, that sounds like a terrible circumstance, since how can someone else know what's right for you? Oh, they can give you some useful advice, and this book will do that too. But since you, not them and not me, live your life, experience your activities, make your friends, feel your pleasures and your pains, no one but you can make the choices that are best for you.

That's really what it means to be an adult: to have the authority to make your own choices and the responsibility to live with them. As a child, your parents, teachers, and maybe others made a lot of choices for you. But as you become an adult, you get to define (or at least influence) your own boundaries and frame the choices as you wish, and then when you've made choices, you, not anyone else, have the opportunity and the obligation to carry them out and live with them.

Choices are so common, we often don't even realize we're making them. Because many are trivial, we don't spend a lot of effort making them. And because many are routine and repetitive, we develop rules of thumb or habits that allow us to make them almost without thinking. Some decisions, however, are pivotal, a big deal, and worth a lot of time and effort.

For now, let's begin with a piece of good news: a lot of the decisions you'll have to make probably don't really matter all that much, so don't fret over them. People may have suggested that some choices are really important that are in fact not all that critical. Take, for example, the choice of which college to attend. If you've decided to go to college and have what it takes to go, just which of quite a large number of schools you select (or that select you) really doesn't make a big difference.

Some schools will be wrong for you—too hard, too easy, too big, or whatever, so you'll want to give the choice some serious attention. But so long as you're selecting from a pool of reasonably appropriate schools, the choice of what college to go to is not so important. The experiences you'll have at one or another will be different, of course, but you can't know ahead of time which will be best or most valuable or most pleasant. Whom you pal around with when you get there, which courses you end up taking, which teacher you get for one or another class, and how diligently you apply yourself to the intellectual and social experiences at your school have a lot more to do with what you get out of college than which school it is you attend. We'll come back to this in the next chapter. However, the decision about whether or not to go to college, as we'll discuss in chapter 2, is a really important decision, one that can make a big difference in your life.

Here's another piece of pretty good news: in many of the big choices in life there's not a single "right" choice with all others being "wrong." Instead, there are better choices or poorer ones, there are some pretty foolish ones or dangerous ones to be sure, and some that are especially appealing—but very seldom is there a uniquely perfect selection. Perhaps there are absolutes in the principles that guide your life and define who you are, but when it comes to selecting this or that level of schooling, job, partner, or whatever, you'll do well to explore your options, come to understand them, and to make a sensible choice by selecting one of the better ones. But don't lose sleep over finding one perfect answer.

Why can't we just avoid making choices? There's just one simple reason: scarcity. You and I have limited resources—limited money, limited time, limited talents, and limited patience. Limits all over the place! If it weren't for scarcity, you could have it all ways, and you wouldn't need to make a choice at all. But since you do face scarcity and do have to make some big choices that can have long-lasting influence, it is a good idea to figure out how best to make wise ones. That's what this book is designed to help you do.

Since choices are so varied, you shouldn't expect to find a simple formula or a single strategy that always produces a good choice; that would trivialize the challenge you face as you consider your decisions. Instead, what you can hope to do is have a framework that gives you some guidance, enables you to consider the important elements of that choice, and helps you avoid overlooking any of these really important elements. That's what we're aiming for here. We'll learn some concepts that will be a big help and explore some facts that can shed some useful light on one or another of the alternatives.

WHAT'S IN A CHOICE?

A good choice will reflect several things: it will reflect your *values*, your *preferences*, your *capabilities*, and your available *opportunities*. That's probably true about most of the choices you make, big and small. Like, what's for lunch? Your values can influence whether you will want a healthy lunch or not; your preferences play a big role in influencing whether it's a salad, some protein, or chips; and if you don't have much cash or credit, your limited capability may be a big factor in your "choice" of what to have for lunch and where to have it. And then, if there's not a shop nearby or a fridge to raid, your preferences and your cash won't matter all that much, so the available opportunities can also define your choice.

Your *values* influence how you behave (or they aren't really the values you live by) and what you want to achieve. There are some values that are pretty universal, like living your life with integrity and having respect and compassion for others. Different religions and various ethical principles teach values that can guide your life, but you are the boss here. You, not some philosopher or your parent, can determine your values and your personal commitment to the principles and beliefs that guide your life.

One of the fun and frightening aspects about becoming an adult is that you will want to consider what values you will live by, what truly matters to you in terms of your own self-esteem, your sense of your deeper self. This can be fun, since talking about your values with friends and people you respect can help clarify what does matter to you. It can also be frightening because, in a sense, your values really do define who you are.

Values aren't innate; you aren't born with them. You've been raised in a family that has some specific values, and because these values are familiar and because you may have seen them serve your family well over your lifetime, you'll probably be inclined to adopt them. But you must decide if those values are the ones you want to guide your behavior as an adult.

Preferences are another of those four elements involved in all your choices. Preferences are not as important as your values; they can change a lot depending on your circumstances at the time. The things you like and the things you don't like are part of your preferences. It's often hard to know where they actually came from. You'll know, however, that you like one sort of music a lot more than another or, say, that your interest in one sport or athletic activity is a lot stronger than that of your friend or your sister. One reason there's so much advertising around is that companies make an effort to inform you about a product and to persuade you that it addresses your preferences.

Preferences vary a lot in their intensity. You may have a preference for action movies over romantic ones, but it might be only a slight edge for this over that. Other preferences can be intense and can really motivate you to take one action or another.

These two elements—your values and your preferences—essentially tell you what you're aiming at, what you're after, what your objective is when you make a choice. If you didn't have any preferences or didn't consider any values important, you couldn't really make a real choice about anything, from your lunch to your life's work, since it wouldn't matter to you if you had no preferences. Values and preferences give you direction. They define your objective. That's a start.

The third element involved in your choices is your *capability*, and that's got a lot to it. One set of capabilities reflects your resources. Money matters. Your access to money is a crucial factor in making some of the choices we'll discuss (and it is a key objective when we consider others). A very different set of capabilities are your skills: the knowledge you've acquired and the personal attributes you bring to the table, like your personality, energy, and appearance. Again, some of the choices that we'll be focusing on—schooling and health habits, especially—greatly influence these capabilities.

The fourth element is your *opportunities*—the options from which you make your choices. You may have been told that you make your own opportunities, and, indeed, that can be so, but only to a degree. There's a reality out there. You were born at a particular time, grew up in some specific location (or several places), and are facing these life decisions in the context of some particular time and space, with options that are good or not so good. Recognizing and assessing the value of the opportunities you have, and understanding what opportunities you are not likely to have, are all part of making sensible decisions that we'll explore in this book.

But you have a lot to do with how well or how poorly things turn out: three of the four elements of your choice are embedded within you, and only one, the opportunities you confront, is outside yourself. That itself can be energizing. While you can't do it all on your own—and if the opportunities aren't there, it doesn't make a lot of difference how "capable" you are—a lot of what matters is within your control.

All of us have heard stories about someone who has had just incredibly bad luck but who picked themselves up, making the most of a bad situation, and turned things around despite setbacks. Everyone will have setbacks in their life. We all meet with disappointment. It's been said that what determines how successful you are in life has a lot more to do with how you handle those disappointments than how you respond to the good things that come along. So get ready to overcome the bad events and to take advantage of the good ones—you will certainly confront both.

Even if you're aware of these four elements (your values, preferences, capabilities, and opportunities), decisions can be difficult. Throughout this book we'll consider choices that are important because they can have a big influence on your life. So, yes, making choices can be somewhat scary. Also, while many of these decisions can be changed later, there's usually a cost to doing so. And when a choice really can't be undone, the stakes are high.

Another reason a lot of choices are so hard is that you often don't know exactly what will happen if you choose one option or another. Uncertainty is a pain. But since it keeps showing up when you think about the sort of decisions we'll talk about, you've got to figure out how to deal with it.

Still another reason some choices are so difficult to make is that they are often interconnected with other important decisions. That makes decision making all the more complicated. What you decide about one choice can affect what you'll want to do about another. Then you won't really know how the first one turns out before you'll face a couple more related choices, which adds to your uncertainty.

Of course, whatever you choose, a lot of stuff happens. Sometimes it may seem that you don't really have any good choices or, for that matter, any influence over how your life goes, no matter how carefully you plan. But even if you can't control everything—and you certainly cannot—it makes a lot of sense to consider your options and to make a choice, even when you can't know everything you'd like to. Punting or avoiding a choice because it's hard is almost never a smart strategy.

The good news is there is some guidance that can help you with these choices, even though it is not the case that this book, or for that matter any advice or guidance from anyone, can tell you what *you* ought to do. Again, your best choice depends on your values, your preferences, your capabilities, and your opportunities. You run your life, not your parents or your friends, not your teachers, mentors, pastor/priest/rabbi, or anyone else. You. It's your life—it's yours to make the most of, and it's you who will suffer when things go wrong or float in the clouds when things go well.

A pretty good word for this aspect of adulthood is "sovereignty": independent authority and the right to govern oneself. Since you have sovereignty over yourself, you should be skeptical when anyone seems to think they can offer you easy answers to some of these life choices—guidance, yes, suggestions, of course, but answers, no. Be careful about accepting anyone else's answers as your own.

Now, of these four elements of choice, we'll focus most of our attention on your capabilities because some of the bigger choices you'll face will help determine just what your capabilities are. We'll also emphasize some of the opportunities you have. By contrast, your values and your preferences will not be a focus here—they lie outside the boundaries of this book, despite being really important to the decisions you make.

That's where the concept of sovereignty comes in. We won't explore where your values come from, and we will only address one preference in particular, something we'll call your time preference, which has a lot to do with the choices we will be discussing. Since we're emphasizing how to make sensible decisions, all four elements will play a role, but most of the concepts we'll use relate to your capabilities and opportunities. And the facts we'll explore are facts about outcomes, not about those basic values or preferences.

THE TOOLS IN THIS BOOK

What we will do in this book is focus on two useful tools: concepts and facts. The *concepts* offer guidance about what to consider when you are facing some of these big decisions. These will be based on what some call the science of choice arising from the fact of scarcity. You don't have to know the science to be able to take advantage of the help it can provide you, just as you don't need to know a lot of biochemistry to take advantage of the prescription medicine your doctor suggests you take. We'll try to benefit from some of the insights of that science but not worry much about where the ideas come from. (A glossary at the back of the book will give you some definitions and names for some of these concepts; if you are especially interested in any of them, there are also suggestions of where you might look them up.)

The second tool, the *facts*, has value if you think knowledge about how others have handled the choices you face might be helpful. Knowledge is affirming and empowering. It can be downright comforting to know what others have decided about these same choices. Together with the concepts, the facts will suggest some of the things you might want to consider and show you the range of options you may have. The facts will also tell us how many people chose one thing or another, and in some instances we will see how those choices worked out for them.

We can get the facts in a couple of ways. For most of the topics discussed, there are general government statistics that are quite informative, and I'll cite a few in each chapter and indicate where you can get more information if you're interested.

Additionally, there's a source of information we'll use that's based on an enormous effort that the federal government, through the U.S. Department of Labor's Bureau of Labor Statistics, has undertaken. It is an ongoing study of the choices made and the resulting outcomes of a large group of people, namely, Americans born in the five-year interval 1980–1984. On January 1, 2000, they were all 15 to 19 years old, so we can call them "Teenage America at the Beginning of the Twenty-First Century." They are often called Millennials, but we will just call them the "1980s Cohort" (a "cohort" is just a group defined by the individual members having something in common—in this case, all those born in a specific five-year interval).

If you are near your early twenties, this 1980s Cohort is just enough ahead of you in age that the choices they made can be instructive. Their choices have, by now, resulted in them likely being your boss on the job, or your rabbi, priest, or minister if you have one, or maybe your teacher, mentor, caseworker, or whatever, and maybe your older cousin or neighbor. So it's interesting to see what choices they made, and in some instances we can also see some of the consequences resulting from those choices.

We don't need to have information from everyone in the cohort to know a lot about their choices and to know it quite accurately. That's the beauty of what we call scientific sampling: a correctly drawn sample from a much larger group, with a careful collection of information, can tell us a lot, very accurately, about the whole group. In our case, we have a scientifically drawn sample of about 9,000 people, and this tells us something about the 18 million people in the United States born in that five-year interval.

The sample was drawn in 1997, and the men and women in the sample have been willing to be interviewed every year in a face-to-face, hour-long interview. If you want to look it up online, the sample is known as the National Longitudinal Survey of Youth, 1997, or "NLSY97." The purpose of the survey was to see what the people in that birth cohort—all 18 million of them—have been up to in terms of their schooling, their employment and earnings, their family life and other major activities and interests. In each chapter of this book, we will make use of this information about the choices these people made as we consider the big decisions you will be facing. There is also an appendix at the back of the book that tells you a lot about the backgrounds and family circumstances of the 1980s Cohort.

LEARNING HOW TO APPLY THE TOOLS

We've got a lot of exciting ground to cover. You'll bring your values and preferences, and we'll discuss the capabilities and opportunities that are relevant to five important life decisions. You'll see that some concepts will be useful in addressing many decisions you'll confront. But not all the concepts are relevant to every choice, of course, and one of the things you may hope to develop is a sense of when one of these concepts is or is not useful in thinking about some decision you face. I'll try to help you develop that sense.

It is quite likely that you have already made a decision, at least a tentative decision, about one or another of the choices we'll focus on in the chapters that follow. That will be helpful, actually, in a couple ways. For one thing, some of the concepts we discuss may have been part of your thinking when you made the choice you made. If so, it can be clarifying to have the concept developed further here so you can use it more effectively in the future. If you did, in fact, incorporate that concept or idea as you made your decision, you will be in great shape to understand its usefulness. Then, if one or another of the concepts introduced here is something you hadn't thought to consider when you made your choice, it is all the more important to come to know that idea, to incorporate it into your thinking in the future so it can be of use to you.

The big decisions we consider in the chapters ahead are ones all young adults face and that will, somehow, get made. You will be making important choices for much of the rest of your life, right up to your old age—if you are so lucky. The scarcity that necessitates choice doesn't go away. Getting good at making decisions and bringing a little more wisdom and good sense to those choices is well worth some effort. Let's now turn to the first of the five life decisions.

TWO | More Schooling?

Why, then the world's mine oyster,
Which I with sword will open.

THE MERRY WIVES OF WINDSOR

If you're in your late teens or early twenties, you've been in school for most of your life. And by now you've already made some key decisions about your education. That makes this choice a good one to begin our discussion. If some of the ideas offer you additional insights, you'll be able to put them to use in your subsequent choices; and, of course, education really never ends—we are learning things throughout our lives.

There are several things that make the decision about how much schooling to get really challenging. Let's list a few of them and then consider each in turn.

First, there are a lot of *costs* connected with schooling. These costs are not just the money that covers tuition and fees, housing, books, and so on. Your time spent at school also has a cost.

Second, a choice about some training beyond high school means thinking about the *present versus the future*. That's an important element of many life decisions. You could decide about schooling completely without thinking about the future. After all, that's the way you decide to go to a concert or to take a trip—it seems like fun. And schooling can be a lot of fun, too. But you can also think about schooling in terms of years far beyond the present. Schooling can affect your life in many ways for many years to come. In the simplest of terms, you can choose to focus on the year in school itself or to focus on those years beyond. That's a key aspect of this decision.

Third, the decision about schooling would be easier if some of the other things you wonder about were already settled. For example, it would help if you knew what your boyfriend is going to do next year, or if that pain in your stomach that's been bothering you gets sorted out, or if that job you've heard about at the company near home is really going to become available in the next few months. Your schooling decision would also be easier if you had a better sense of just how it will affect you—the sort of job you could expect, the sort of lifestyle you might adopt, the sort of friendships you'd have, and the sort of things you'd learn about. There's lots of *uncertainty* about this choice, so we'll discuss how to deal with it.

Finally, you are aware that some folks have it easy when it comes to paying for school while others have it really tough, much more so than you, probably. But money isn't the only thing that differs a lot among people as they consider how much schooling to get. There's a lot of variation in a whole range of things that can influence this choice: health, personality, athletic ability, intelligence, energy, optimism, and on and on. *Inequality* of all sorts abounds.

The decision about whether or not to go for more schooling can be bewildering. The thing is, this isn't the only really complicated choice faced by a young person around age 20—decisions about a career, about moving out of your parents' (or parent's) home, about how serious to be about that boyfriend, and many more choices are all complicated and frighteningly interconnected.

The choices about education and training arise at a lot of different stages of schooling. People differ in just what level of schooling raises the issue of whether or not to go on for more or what sort of schooling to seek. For some, completing high school and attending college is practically a no-brainer, while for others, for all sorts of good reasons, there's a tough decision to make about completing high school or about going to a trade school or a two-year community college or a four-year college. Beyond college as well, some choose to go for advanced degrees and certification in all sorts of professions. We'll talk the issues through by focusing on the choice about whether to go to a four-year college, but the same issues arise—costs, weighing the present versus the future, uncertainty, and inequality—whether you are considering dropping out of high school, seeking a vocational training, or getting a two- or four-year college degree or postgraduate training. There's not one right answer for everyone: For some, it really wouldn't be wise to borrow the money to pay tuition and fees to go for post-high-school training; for others, it would be a very good thing to do. You'll want to consider your circumstances when you choose.

There are some useful concepts that can guide these schooling decisions. They can make the elements of your choices a lot clearer and will help you make sure that the key issues get enough attention as part of your decision making. There are also a lot of useful facts about schooling and its outcomes. Let's go through these four issues about schooling that make the decision a hard one, and let's consider how some of these concepts help guide the choice. And along the way we'll look at a few facts.

PRICES

College takes money, lots of it. And the price of different colleges seems to vary quite a bit. So what should you do? Prices typically reflect two things: the cost of producing an item and the importance or value people put on it. Maybe you've heard it said that many things come down to "supply and demand." A seller of most any item—from a rubber ball to a college education—has costs to cover in producing the product and offering to sell it to you—that's the "supply" side. But then the buyers get just as much say in what the price actually is, because if they don't value that product and don't want to buy it at the price offered, it won't be sold. If that happens, the price will need to come down until folks do value it enough to pay that lower price. Otherwise the seller will discover she can't actually sell the product at a price that covers all her costs. When that happens, the product disappears from the market. This happens all the time—for example, when a restaurant in your neighborhood goes out of business or when one cell phone or one line of tennis shoes replaces another one in the marketplace.

Often you'll hear that the price reflects the quality of the product, so a higher price implies it is a better one than a lower-priced one. That may often be true, but it doesn't mean that the higher-priced product is best for everyone. Think of all the extras on the things you bought recently that you never use—it would be silly to spend a lot of extra money to buy a more expensive camera, car, computer, or education just because it has a lot of extra options that you don't really value.

Some colleges cost more because they have extra programs or specialties or sports that you don't care about—their prices reflect extra costs of producing the school experience they offer, which may have a lot of value for someone else, but those costly extras may not be relevant for you. When you buy a product, you express your preferences. However, you may need to spend some time looking for just the right combination of things to satisfy your preferences.

When it comes to schooling beyond high school, there are lots of options. There are vocational education programs that focus narrowly—but effectively—on skills useful in some particular job, like cosmetology or welding or salesmanship. There are programs that offer certification that take one or two years to complete, and other schools that offer a two-year associate degree, while still others offer a more common four-year general education degree like a bachelor of arts (BA) or bachelor of science (BS) degree. Colleges typically offer one degree only, like a BA degree, while universities offer several degrees, usually including some more advanced than a BA, such as an MA, a PhD, or an MD.

The size of the school, the number of courses and concentrations offered, and many other elements of what a college or university offers all affect its price. This includes things like the quality of its faculty and its facilities such as labs, libraries, housing, sports centers, and other components of the experience of going to school there.

To reduce the bewildering array of options you need to consider, you should have a clear sense of what matters most to you as a prospective student—is it some particular area of study like a creative writing program or Mandarin language courses, or is it the size of the student body, the availability of some sport program, or the location of the school? Knowing which elements of your choice matter a lot and which matter only a little can make choosing a lot easier. Price is a guide to the nature of what's offered, but you need to look into what the price is reflecting and then think about whether what that school offers is what you want.

There's another aspect of the price of college: the fact that the price is so high that many families can't afford to pay it. Now, that's also true of buying a house to live in, buying a car, or maybe paying for a wedding or a major vacation. For a really big purchase, it is often necessary either to save up for a few years before buying the item or to borrow up front and pay off the loan over several years to come. We'll set this aspect of choosing a college to one side for a while and come back to it.

TIME COSTS

Another cost of going to college is time. In fact, if you consider that all those months of schooling are months you could have been working and earning wages or doing something else of value to you, tuition is typically only about half of the whole cost. The wages forgone are just as much a part of the price of college as are the tuition and room-and-board expenses. The time cost is an important part of the total cost in many types of purchases. It is often called an "opportunity cost" since it reflects the value of the opportunity you give up by spending your time in this activity.

If you think of the whole cost of a year of college as the price of tuition and fees plus the value of your time spent in school, that sum reflects the value of all the resources expended in getting you a year of schooling. Some of those resources are provided by the school, and these are paid for by the tuition and fees. Other resources are actually provided by you when you spend your time taking classes and preparing coursework. That's one of the functions of a price—it shows the whole time and money cost of producing a year of your schooling. Oh, did you wonder if there's a difference between the "cost" and the "price"? Cost generally means the value of the resources used to produce the product—in this case, those resources used by both the school and by you, since producing your education is really a cooperative endeavor. Price is what it takes to acquire the product from its producer or whoever owns it. In most cases, the price and cost are essentially the same, but there are lots of products for which that's not so because the seller can insist on a price higher than the cost (if, for example, he is a monopolist) or because someone is willing to pay a part of the cost so the price you face is lower than the cost (if, for example, the state wants to encourage you to go to college so it offers in-state tuition at a level that's below the cost of providing the education).

PRESENT-FUTURE

The second aspect of the decision about college involves time in another sense—today versus tomorrow. You've probably heard that schooling is like an investment—you pay a price up front, and you get a "return" on that investment over the years ahead. That's part of it, but let's recall that going to college can also be a lot of fun. Many of the courses you take are actually really interesting, and knowing stuff is itself quite satisfying. Add to that the fact that you'll be spending your time with a lot of people who share your interests and capabilities. As many who have gone to college will tell you, it can be one of the best times of your life. You'll probably meet some of your best lifetime friends in college, and many people find their life mate during their college years. It's a time for a lot of exploration of what's important to you, of what sort of life you want to lead, and what sort of impact you would like to have on the world.

So some of the cost of going to college is offset by the enjoyment of being there, inspired by new ideas and by mentors and teachers, exploring what's important to you, and experiencing new opportunities. That part of the cost of college is just like the cost of an evening at the concert or the cost of a week's vacation, since you pay the price and you get some real enjoyment from the experience you have.

Don't forget this aspect of the choice about college—too often the decision becomes bogged down in whether you can afford it, which school to apply to, or whether you will get into the school of your choice. In that case, you might forget to notice just how lucky you are that you are at an age and stage of life when it is acceptable to go absorb a lot of exciting new experiences, learn a lot that will bring you satisfaction for years, and acquaint yourself with friends who will last a lifetime.

So now let's consider that notion of "investing" in college. We've just said that college has a cost and that it can be a lot of fun. So why isn't the decision about going to college just the same as the decision about, say, buying a car or a season ticket to your favorite profes-

Table 2.1: Weekly Earnings of Full-Time Wage and Salary
Workers, by Schooling Level (men and women, age 25 and over)

Level of Schooling	Median Weekly Earnings
Less than high school diploma	$488
High school diploma	668
Some college or associate's degree	761
Bachelor's degree	1,101
Advanced degree	1,386

Source: Bureau of Labor Statistics, "Usual Weekly Earnings of Wage and
Salary Workers: Fourth Quarter 2014," January 21, 2015, table 9 (based
on 2014 CPS), www.bls.gov/news.release/archives/wkyeng_01212015.pdf.

sional team's home games? Investments are different. You invest in
something because you expect that it will pay you back more than it
cost, and the extra payment is a "return" on that investment. Since
you can invest in a lot of different things, you'll want to make your
investment in the things that seem to offer the highest return. Different investments pay you back in different ways. Investments in
education pay you back in a higher wage rate or earnings. Let's look
at some facts to see that this is, in general, true. Then we'll consider
why it is so and ask what it implies for you.

Table 2.1 shows the average weekly earnings of full-time workers with different levels of schooling. The first two lines of the table
show that those who have less than a high school diploma earn $488
for a week's work, while those with a high school diploma earn $668.
Then for each additional level of schooling, average weekly earnings
rise. It may seem obvious, but let's consider why.

Firms produce goods and services and sell them at a price that
covers their costs, including the owner's own efforts. Those costs, in
turn, include the payments to his workers and for the machinery and
buildings he uses, for raw materials, for the services he buys such as
IT support, and for all the other resources he needs like any patents
he relies on or any required insurance. The wages he pays his workers reflect the value of their contribution to his production. So he
pays higher wages to the workers who make a bigger contribution to
his production—they may be faster at doing the job, or more knowledgeable about key decisions that need to be made, or more depend-
able, or any number of other things that make them, at the end of the
day, more productive.

The facts about weekly wages seen in the table suggest that a college graduate can produce more than twice as much value in a week on the job as the high school dropout can. Yes, there's a lot more involved, but the essential nature of the relationship is clear: more schooling means greater production, and that means a higher wage. It really is like other investments: you pay up front and buy the schooling, thereby acquiring the skills that make you more productive on the job, and you later earn a higher salary.

The higher salary is the return on the investment you made in your schooling. And just like machinery and buildings used in production, the skill or knowledge acquired by schooling is "capital." Since this schooling capital is embedded in the person, in you, it is considered "human capital." It has real cost and real value.

Studies have calculated the rate of return on an investment in college, taking account of all its costs and the higher earnings. The facts suggest that a college education pays a rate of return of between 10% and 15% for most people who get a college degree. This means that most people who invest in college make all that investment back, plus another 10–15% of that investment over their lifetime. The rate of return has varied from decade to decade, but it has been that high for a very long time and, thanks to all the technology afoot, it's been on the high end of that range in recent years.

Now, it seems that a good rate of return on a college education is likely to continue to be so for decades to come. However, that does not mean that everyone should go to college, and it surely doesn't mean that the investment is guaranteed to pay off for everyone who does go. The actual payoff depends on a lot of things: these range from how well prepared you are for college, your native ability, your college major, and the effort you put forth. It also depends on how many hours and how much effort you put into the job after you're hired as well as the general state of the economy when you finish college.

What the payoff will be for you is one of those things that's uncertain, so we'll talk about this shortly. But another thing is that whatever the payoff or "rate of return" on the investment is, your decision also should depend on what your cost is for getting the money necessary to go to college! That's where the issue of inequality comes up, and we'll discuss that below as well. First, let's notice a few things about this "human capital investment," which is different from a lot of other investments you might consider—in stocks and bonds or in real estate, for example.

For one thing, unlike a savings account or even a piece of real estate, this investment isn't easy to sell off—it's not what's called a "liquid" investment. This investment in embedded in you. If you decided you didn't want it after you got it, you can't just sell it or get your money back from the school like you might do with a share of stock or an automobile. The investment in schooling gives you skills, knowledge, habits, attitudes, and capabilities that have value, which pay off, but they become part of you. That's really different from an investment in a few shares of stock.

Another thing about this investment is that in order to get a high return, you have to make use of the investment. If you buy shares of a mutual fund and just let them sit idle for several years, they'll likely increase in value without you doing anything about it. That's not the way it works with an investment in schooling. You have to put those new skills, habits, and knowledge to work for the investment to pay off. On the bright side, there's evidence that the more you use your newly acquired skills, the better they get—so the payoff actually increases the more you use your investment.

If you think about it, that's one reason people with more schooling are typically in better health than those with less schooling: to be able to work and earn that return on their investment in schooling, they need to be healthy! Those with more education have more reason, or a bigger incentive, to avoid habits that might harm their health and impair their ability to work. We'll come back to this in chapter 6 when we consider decisions about health.

Yet another thing that's different about this investment is that since it is embedded in you and has payoff by affecting how productive you are, it makes a lot of sense to invest in schooling at an early age. That way, you have your whole lifetime to get the benefit of the investment. You can't pass along the asset (your skills and know-how) to your loved ones when you die. The investment comes to an end at that point, so you'll want to get it as early in your lifetime as feasible.

If you'll grant me a bit too much poetic license here, we might think of education as your "sword" in the quotation at the beginning of this chapter—the knowledge and skills acquired through schooling enable you to take up opportunities for productive pursuit that come along—opening your oyster, so to speak (assuming you like oysters!).

We said that the investment in education pays you back in a higher wage and that's true—but it is really only part of the story. There's also evidence that the skills you acquire in school affect your "productivity" outside the labor market. If schooling makes you more productive in getting a task accomplished on the job, it can also help you in the same way at home—in deciding what products you buy or the terms you negotiate with vendors. If schooling makes you more skillful in using machinery on the job, it probably also makes you more skillful in using the machines you have around the house, like your computer. If schooling helps you learn new stuff on the job more easily or quicker, or gives you a broader basis for deciding how to handle a problem on the job, it probably does the same thing for you on your days not at work, on weekends and on vacations. So the payoff in terms of the whole impact on your life from an investment in schooling may be much greater than only the potentially larger paycheck.

Speaking of a paycheck, there's another part of the "return" on an investment in more education: a greater likelihood of being able to find and keep a job. The year 2012 was a rather bad year for finding employment in the United States, but as table 2.2 shows, it was much harder for those who had less education.

We see that the rate of unemployment (or the percentage of people who can't find a job among those who can and want to work) was nearly three times higher for high school dropouts than for those with a four-year college degree. It was higher for those with less schooling, across the board. That was so in 2012 when the overall unemployment rate was high (6.8%), and it was also true a couple years later when the overall rate was much lower (5%).

There are several reasons why it is harder to find a job if you have less schooling, and we'll talk about them in the next chapter. But if you are considering more schooling, it is an important fact that in economic recessions, the less educated tend to get laid off more quickly and to have a lot more difficulty finding a new job.

Table 2.2: U.S. Unemployment Rate, by Schooling Level, 2012 and 2014

Level of Schooling	Unemployment Rate	
	2012	2014
Less than high school diploma	12.4%	9.0%
High school diploma	8.3	6.0
Some college, no degree	7.7	6.0
Associate's degree	6.2	4.5
Bachelor's degree	4.5	3.5
Master's degree	3.5	2.8
Professional degree	2.1	1.9
Doctoral degree	2.5	2.1
Overall	6.8	5.0

Sources: Bureau of Labor Statistics, "Earnings and Unemployment Rates by Educational Attainment," www.bls.gov/emp/ep_chart_001.htm. 2012 data on line 12, July 2013; 2014 data on line 11, April 2015.

Let's return to our discussion of time. If the reason you go on for more schooling is those higher earnings, you'll want to think about that in terms of a trade-off between the present and the future. Suppose you are considering going to a school that will cost you $20,000 for one year, and suppose you can pay that amount without borrowing any of it. That means that right now you have $20,000 that you could enjoy spending on things you like now. Or you could invest that $20,000 in a year of college and later in your life, as you work in your chosen profession, you can expect to get back more than your $20,000—the "more" is the return on that investment, which we mentioned above has been around 10–15%.

But you get it back later—years later. So you have to wait. You have to give up that money now in exchange for getting more later when you are older. You can choose to have something you want now, or you can choose to wait, to invest, and thus to have more later.

One element of your choice, then, depends on your willingness to wait. Think about that: how do you feel about it? Sooner is better, after all; we can probably all agree on that. Why wait to enjoy something you can enjoy today, right? But then if you can have more later, it may be more appealing to wait. It will depend, at least in part, on how long you need to wait and how much more you'll get if you do wait. The technical term for how willing you are to wait is "time preference."

Most of us have a time preference for the present over the future. We differ, however, in how much of a preference we have for now versus later. As a general rule, folks who have a lower time preference for now (that is, those who are willing to wait) have a better life overall—better in terms of higher income, a healthier life, more stable relationships, and in a lot of other ways. That's part of why parents and mentors are keen on investing in schooling and discouraging behaviors that seem attractive today but have harmful effects on future outcomes. Time preference is a big deal.

In the early 1970s there was a famous study, now known as the marshmallow test, that explored at what age in children's lives they develop the capacity to control their behavior "today" in order to get a payoff "tomorrow." Each nursery school kid in the experiment could have either one marshmallow (or some pretzels or a cookie) as she sat alone in a room for a few minutes, or if she didn't eat the marshmallow before the adult returned, she was told she would be given two marshmallows—but to get the two, she had to wait and not eat the one that was just sitting there in front of her.

Well, some children ate the one marshmallow, and some waited and got the payoff of two—that's a pretty big payoff for only waiting a few minutes, you might think. The professor who ran the study then wrote about the factors that seemed to be linked to the kids who waited for the payoff and those who did not.[1] What makes this study famous, however, is that the professor contacted the same kids years later. Those who had waited for the two marshmallows, back when they were in nursery school, turned out to be "more competent" as adolescents (as judged by their parents) and to have higher SAT scores, ultimately higher levels of schooling, and generally more successful lives.[2] No one thinks there was some magic ingredient in that second marshmallow! There was something about being able to wait, to delay gratification when it seemed like a good thing to do. Those who chose to wait turned out to do better later in life.

We can make the point about your actions today versus your options tomorrow in another way: it is as true looking backward as looking forward. What you did, how you behaved, and what choices you made when you were younger have already had an impact on your circumstances today. That will continue to be true tomorrow and for the rest of your life. Decisions you made about sports when you were a little kid have had an influence on your athletic proficiency today. Decisions you made about how hard you worked on homework in elementary school have had an impact on your grades and progress through high school (and will continue to have influence in college). The things you took up as your hobbies or interests a few years ago have become areas in which you are more proficient and more informed today. Friends you made and worked hard to develop really close friendships with are likely to be among your closest friends now.

The negative side of this works just as relentlessly: if you engaged in highly risky or socially harmful behaviors or activities when you were younger, that probably has had an impact on your life today. But don't despair: you are relatively young and able to do things now that will make your life better in the future, and you, we'll hope, can work to undo some of the repercussions of past choices that you may now wish you had not made.

Life can be described as a little bit like putty and clay: at first, it's malleable, adjustable, and pliable, much like putty. As you age, many of your options and your capabilities become more limited, less adjustable, and a bit more rigid—more like a piece of baked clay that reflects the choices you made earlier. There's no better example of that than the decision you made when you were younger about practicing piano, learning Spanish, batting, or whatever. If you spent a lot of time working on that skill back then, you are most likely a lot better at that activity now. It's harder as you get older to get as good as you might have been if you had practiced more when you were younger. So it behooves you to think about the long-term effects of choices today, since you'll be living with the results and you won't be able to change things as easily when you get older.

All this is a part of this issue of "time preference." The evidence is so compelling that folks are better off if they don't have too strong a preference for the present over the future, that this is one of the few places in this book where it may be appropriate to violate the rule about not giving advice about what choice to make. I think there's enough evidence to warrant saying that it would be good if you try rather hard to put more importance on the future and less importance on the present—to have a lower time preference for the present.

If you make an effort to pay more attention to the likely future results of the things you do today, this can become a habit. You will make a lot of choices based on that habit. But you get to decide. No one else can tell you how much you value the present over the future. Give it some serious thought.

UNCERTAINTY AND RISK

Something that makes the choice about going to college a bit scary is that you don't really know just what the experience will bring or just how it will affect you. There's a lot of uncertainty surrounding the decision. In fact, there is generally a lot of uncertainty surrounding most of the big decisions in life—where to live, with whom to live, what sort of job to seek, what sort of groups to join, if you should have children, and on and on. Uncertainty is, unfortunately, a fact of life. One of the main challenges of becoming a mature and responsible adult is learning how to deal with it.

The first point to remember about uncertainty is that it's not a good strategy to avoid making decisions because of it. On the other hand, it's also not a good idea to ignore uncertainty when it's there. There are many degrees of uncertainty—some things are only a little bit uncertain, while other things are wildly uncertain. Similarly, some uncertainty matters a lot, and some doesn't really matter so much. In terms of steps you can take when faced with uncertainty, there are three useful strategies: (1) you can do things that will help you understand and assess the uncertainty; (2) you can often take steps to actually reduce the uncertainty; (3) when you can't reduce the uncertainty further, you can frequently take steps to minimize its impact.

Take a pretty simple example first: suppose you are considering buying a used car from a neighbor. Since it's a used car, the uncertainty lies in whether it will run dependably. To address this uncertainty, you can (1) get a better idea of the amount of uncertainty by asking a lot of questions about the car's history: Has it ever been in a major accident? Can you see its service records from the dealer's checkups and repairs? That way you can acquire information that will let you know about the uncertainty you face with that car. You can also (2) take steps that can actually reduce the uncertainty by asking the neighbor to have the car serviced and those tires and brake linings replaced before you buy it. Finally, you can (3) protect yourself from the risk of a bad outcome by buying some insurance or taking out a warranty guarantee against some of the things that might go wrong with the car.

These actions are likely to affect the cost somewhat, but it is often prudent to spend some money now to lower the risk of a later outcome that can be much more costly than the cost of searching for and fixing problems or insuring against that risk. (This touches on our earlier discussion of time preference.)

When it comes to the choice about more schooling, there's uncertainty about a lot of different things. You can search for information about the schools of interest to you. You can find out what programs they offer, what the schools will expect of you academically, what sort of students your classmates will be. You can look into possible fellowships or internships that can offset some of the costs, et cetera. You can also get information about the training program or the college major you are considering.

Beyond looking into potential schools, you can find information about the nature of jobs that require various skills, what they pay, how much turnover there has been in those jobs, where those jobs are located, how easy it is for workers with the skills you are considering to find jobs, and so forth. You can also set up informational interviews with representatives of the firms you might like to work for to determine what suggestions they have about relevant training programs. You can ask which schools they hire most new workers from.

For every piece of information you get about the various elements that are uncertain, the better equipped you'll be in making the decision about the right level of schooling, the right school, and the right concentration or major for you.

Here's a great strategy for making a sensible choice when there's a lot of uncertainty: make a list of the things you are uncertain about, then go after each item on that list in turn, using the three steps discussed above. (1) Find out all you can about each item on your list, (2) ask yourself if there's a way to lower the uncertainty, and then (3) think about how to hedge against the worst possible outcomes presented by the remaining uncertainty. You'll probably still have much that you don't feel you are certain about, but the range of what you don't know can be substantially reduced.

Also a good practice is to do another exercise: begin by describing three or four possible outcomes about which you are uncertain. For example, if you are uncertain about the friendships you'll make and whether you will fit into the social life of the school, describe for yourself outcomes A and B and C and D. Think of A as about as good of an outcome as you can imagine at that school, with several new really close friendships and a truly joyful social network of classmates and activities. Think about B as a reasonably good outcome, maybe on par with your most recent year of high school if it was pretty good but not over-the-top great. Think about C as a disappointing outcome with only a couple friends, limited but tolerable parties and extracurricular life on weekends, and a bit boring overall. And think about D as about as bad as you think is at all likely (not as bad as you can imagine, only as bad, realistically, as you think it might be).

Then do three things with that list of possible outcomes related to that one uncertainty. On a scale of 1 (really awful and not something you could put up with for long) to 5 (really terrific and as good as you can hope it could be), put a value on each of those four outcomes: maybe A is a 5, B is a 4, C is a 3, and D is a 2, since for you this particular issue isn't all that terrible, even at its worst, so a score of 1 seems too low here.

Next, quite separately ask yourself how likely each of the four outcomes is, as best you can judge. Perhaps you'll say that A isn't actually very likely, maybe only about 10% likely, whereas B seems pretty much the most likely outcome as far as you can tell, so you might give it a 70%. Then maybe C would get a 15% because you think it is more likely than A but still not all that likely, since you'll have some wiggle room and can choose your friends slowly and carefully. Considering that awful outcome, D, which isn't really likely but is in truth a possibility, maybe you give it a probability of 5%. (Notice that the sum of those probabilities is 100%, and you can adjust them among the four possible outcomes so the sum is always 100%.)

Next, multiply those probabilities times the scale score you gave each of those outcomes and get the sum of them. In the example here that means for A: 5 × .10 = .50; for B: 4 × .70 = 2.8; for C: 3 × .15 = .45; and for D: 2× .05 = .10. The sum of all four is 3.85. You can think of that number as what you expect to be the outcome you experience on that one element of uncertainty at that one school. You now have a handle on this one aspect of that one school—you've a sense of what to expect socially—and can compare it to other aspects and other schools.

You can do this for each of the schools you are considering separately. You can do this for other types of uncertainty, too, like how you expect to do in that school academically, or how you'll afford the costs of that school, and whatever else is uncertain. You can similarly place a number on the aspects of each school that don't have any uncertainty for you but are also important to you. When you've done this and you compare these numbers across schools and across risks, some may jump out at you as particularly troublesome or especially attractive. That can help you make your decision. You'll *not* want to just add up all the scores for each school and compare them since that would place equal importance on each element of uncertainty. Instead, keep the scores separate and consider each one in turn. If some element is especially important to you, pay special attention to its scores across schools.

There's another uncertainty about going to college that is, I think, much overrated as a problem but it is, indeed, uncertain: will you get into the college of your choice? This is a case of a lot of uncertainty, but it also has a lot less importance than many folks seem to suggest. There are lots of excellent colleges out there, and you can have a fine experience and learn a great deal in many of them. Now, it's worth learning as much as you can about what various schools offer so you can make an informed and reasonable choice for yourself. You do need to "hedge" your bet a bit by applying to several schools, with maybe one or two that are a bit of a stretch for you and another one or two that are relatively sure things in terms of acceptance.

But in the final analysis, which school you go to among the several you find that can serve your interests matters a lot less than the choices you make once you get there—about the courses you take, the effort you put into your academic work, the friends you choose, the lifestyle you lead, and more. Don't let the uncertainty about getting in that one "right" school get in your way of making a sensible choice and enjoying the process of imagining yourself in this school or that one.

Another thing: no school is perfect! You'll not find any college or training program that offers just exactly what you would like, at just the right cost, in just the right location, with just the right student housing, and so on. You might as well get used to that fact since it is in general true of schools, jobs, life partners, houses, religions, and most everything else. It's also true about you—perfection is very unlikely, and it doesn't last very long if you do experience it. Getting used to imperfection is a part of growing up. Recognize that the imperfections are part of life. They offer opportunities to show yourself that you are strong enough to rise above them and to have a worthy and good life nonetheless.

PAYING THE PRICE

The final issue we listed at the outset about deciding whether to go on for more schooling was the observation that some people have easy access to the money needed to pay college tuition while others really have no chance of getting that money easily. That doesn't mean that only those who have the money should go to college. Nevertheless, accessing the money needed to attend college is an important issue, and there are choices to be made about how best to obtain it.

If the cost of borrowing the money is too high, it may not be a good idea to make the investment, despite a good "return." We'll explore that.

There are a couple of issues here that are really different. One is how best to secure the funds to go to college, and the other is more basic still: why it is that some families have the money readily available to pay for college and others don't. Let's consider them in turn.

For a big expenditure like paying for college, there are two ways to go if you don't have the money readily available: you can wait while you accumulate the money over time by saving, or you can borrow and pay the loan back over time.

The advantage of waiting and saving is that you earn the interest going along instead of paying the interest to the lender; the disadvantage is that you need to wait for several years for the savings to accumulate. If you were considering buying a big item that is essentially for your enjoyment, for "consumption," most advisers will counsel waiting and saving before you make the purchase. But for an investment with a good return, it usually *doesn't* make sense to wait. It would probably make more sense to borrow the funds, make the investment, and begin getting that return on the investment— so long as the return is greater than the cost of the loan.

That would be true for other types of investments as well, for instance, if you were considering establishing a small restaurant or some other business. This principle applies even more so for the investment in your human capital. After all, this investment is made in your skills and knowledge, so the sooner you make it, the longer in your lifetime you'll be able to use that investment, and therefore the rate of return may be higher if you make the investment earlier. The basic issue here is pretty straightforward: if you have concluded that for you a college education is likely to pay a return like that 10–15% on future earnings mentioned earlier, then if you can borrow at a rate of interest lower than the rate of return you'll get from college, it's a wise thing, financially, to borrow the money for college. But be sure you know what the rate of interest is on the loan you take out, and be realistic in assessing the rate of return you think will apply to you if you go to college.

One of the things that's different about a loan to cover the cost of education compared to a loan to buy a house or to start a business is that issue of "liquidity" mentioned earlier. If you borrow to buy a house or to buy machines for your new business and then later can't make the payments on your loan, the lender can take the house or the machinery—it is "collateral." That gives you something to bargain with and gives the lender some assurances. You can't do that with your education—if you can't make the payments on the loan, the lender can't take the skills, knowledge, and experiences you acquired at school instead of the money you owe. And you, too, can't sell these things off and get the money to repay the loan. That's one reason why there are programs in which the government "guarantees" some student loans so you and the lender can, in fact, think of a loan to pay for college in the same way as in a commercial loan. Consequently, the interest rate that the lender charges is lower (or should be!), and this helps make it prudent for you to make the investment in your education.

Here are a couple more things to consider about the decision to take out a loan to pay for your schooling. While the return on that human capital investment is high for many high school graduates, and surely is a wise investment for many, one thing the research has shown is that making half the investment doesn't result in half as much impact on your wage. There's a "premium" to finishing the schooling you set out to get. If you go to a four-year college, it is pretty important, in terms of that investment, that you complete the four years and earn the degree. The job market seems to be leery about the signal given by starting a four-year program and not finishing, so you would need to stick with it.

Another thing is that not all college majors are equally good at boosting your salary. There's an important second decision you'd need to make along the way about the particular skills you acquire in college. This doesn't imply that you should only take courses that are likely to give you job-market skills if you're interested in something else. After all, we noted that college is fun and prepares you for a lot more than your occupation. It also offers you the chance to learn about things well beyond your job, to get exposed to ideas, histories, facts, and ways of thinking that will give you satisfaction throughout your life as a worker, yes, but also as a parent, a citizen, a life partner, and an adult.

So don't limit yourself, but then do realize that your choices of courses and concentrations in your education will, in fact, offer you skills in some but not all occupations. You need to give some attention to just how the skills you acquire impact your job prospects, especially if you have student loans you need to repay.

Finally, let's return to that deeper question posed above: Why is it that families differ so much in their ability to pay for their children's college? What explains all this economic inequality? Let's make one pass at this now and return to the question in later chapters as well. Schooling plays a key role. The knowledge and skills that one acquires going to school are a primary factor influencing one's productivity as a worker, so it has a big impact on earnings. That's as true for your parents' generation as it is for you, and this implies that families in which the parents have more education typically—not always, by any means—have higher earnings and have acquired greater savings over their lifetime. In some ways, that's unfair—those families who "have" get more, and those who "have not" are left behind. It's a little like playing basketball with the "make it, take it" rule.

But from another perspective, those who made the effort, studied diligently, and went on for more schooling now enjoy the payoff of enough wealth to provide schooling for their children. There are lots of exceptions to this observation. Some of your financially better-off friends may not have highly educated parents, but instead have parents who took exceptional risks in their careers that turned out well, or just had amazing luck, or worked unbelievably hard and long to sacrifice and save the funds needed for your buddy's college tuition. Still, we can confidently say—based on a lot of evidence—that one of the most reliable characteristics of those parents who have enough money to pay for college is that they got a good education themselves.

Those who have not acquired enough schooling or sufficient knowledge to be able to make skilled efforts in the job market, to "produce enough value," are unable to earn a high wage and are much less likely to be able to pay the costs of college for their children. As technology has continued to advance and machines have taken over more of the routine and the (literally) heavy-lifting jobs, there are fewer jobs for unskilled brawn or for doing routine, lower-paying tasks. More and more jobs that are available require advanced understanding of mathematics and communication skills. Without sufficient schooling, those more demanding and better-paying jobs are just not attainable. There are certainly exceptions, but for the vast majority of adults, those with the least schooling have the lowest income.

Several decades ago the federal government declared a "war on poverty," and one of the primary weapons in that war—one of the main ways to help people get out of poverty—was education. There's been a lot of success in that "war," although our society certainly can't declare victory; yet few would argue that education isn't one of the most effective means for reducing poverty.

What this all means for you is this: First, the overwhelming evidence of a close link between education levels and earnings should convince you that schooling is, indeed, an effective vehicle for preparing yourself to earn relatively more in your work life. Second, it may be motivating to consider that years from now, when you have a child about the age to decide whether he wants to go to college, your own decision now will very likely have an impact on your ability to help him pay for it.

THE 1980S COHORT'S SCHOOLING CHOICES

We've discussed several important ideas that can inform your schooling choice. Before moving on, we will also look at the schooling choices made recently by one entire generation, the men and women in the 1980s Cohort who were teenagers at the start of the new century. Seeing what schooling decisions these Millennials made and how their choices are working out through their late twenties can provide some facts that may be useful as you make your own decision.

One of the most effective ways to look at and learn from huge amounts of information is through tables. To be sure you understand how to read the tables below, let's go through a couple of them in some detail and then, as we present tables in subsequent chapters, you'll be able to go through them yourself.

In table 2.3, panel A organizes the information we have into different levels of grade point average (GPA) in high school. The first column of numbers (or, vertical list, in this case called "Population") reports on the whole cohort, that is, *everyone* born in all five years, 1980 through 1984. The rows (horizontal) match up with each specific level of GPA. The number in each cell tells us the percentage of all the people within that column's group that has that row's specific level. So the first number in the upper left, 10.2, means that, among everyone in the whole cohort, a little more than 10% had a high school GPA below a C average. The number below that, 12.1, tells us

Table 2.3: High School GPAs and the Likelihood of a College Degree by Age 30

	Population	Whites	Blacks	Hispanics	Females	Males
Panel A: Grade Point Average (GPA) in High School						
< 2.0 (below a C average)	10.2%	9.1%	13.6%	12.1%	6.8%	13.3%
2.0 (C average)	12.1	10.3	17.1	14.6	8.6	15.4
2.1–2.9 (B to C average)	24.8	22.2	32.7	30.1	22.5	26.9
3.0 (B average)	16.5	16.9	14.7	16.5	16.5	16.5
3.1–3.9 (A to B average)	22.5	24.1	17.8	19.5	27.1	18.1
4.0 (all A's)	13.9	17.5	4.1	7.2	18.3	9.8
Panel B: The Individual's Estimate (in 1997) of the Likelihood of Having a Four-Year College Degree by Age 30						
No chance (zero)	6%	6%	4%	5%	4%	7%
Small chance (1–25%)	7	6	9	10	6	9
Modest chance (26–75%)	30	28	29	39	25	34
Very good chance (76–99%)	22	24	15	18	21	23
Certainty (100%)	35	35	43	28	43	28

Source: The 1980s Cohort.

that another 12% had a C average, 24.8% had a C to B average, and so on—almost 14% (13.9%) had all A's in their high school record. So there are some pretty smart and hardworking people here, as you'd expect, and there are a lot with more ordinary grades.

The next column over tells us the same information for the white men and women only. The third column tells us the facts for black men and women only. We see that a little more than 9% of whites had a GPA below a C and a larger percentage, 17.5%, had all A's. Each successive column tells us about a specific group, either a race/ethnic group or a gender group.

Everyone in the whole cohort can only be in one of the columns labeled "Whites," "Blacks," or "Hispanics." (If the person could actually be in a couple of these groups, there was a procedure for deciding which to put that person in, so these three groups are mutually exclusive—no one is in more than one of these three columns.) That's also true for the final two columns showing the GPAs for females and for males separately. (Who had better grades in this cohort, the females or the males?) The first column that has everyone in the whole population includes some people who don't fit in any of the race/ethnic groups, such as Asians and American Indians who are in the population but too few to allow us to have a column telling about them alone.

The second panel in table 2.3, panel B, is a bit odd, so let's go through it as well. In the first year of the survey, 1997, the adolescents were asked a lot of questions about what they expected to happen to them in the future. Those who were at least 14 years old were asked: "Now think ahead to when you turn 30 years old. What is the percentage chance that you will have a four-year college degree by the time you turn 30?" If they thought they had no chance of getting a college degree, they could of course answer with a percentage as low as zero, or if they thought it was absolutely certain they'd get a college degree, they could answer 100%, with the others answering somewhere in between.

Panel B of the table tells us what their expectations were about having a college degree by age 30; they did in fact range from zero all the way to 100% among these respondents. Across the whole group, only 6% thought the chance of getting that degree was zero, and a whopping 35% thought the chance was a certainty. Overall, they were quite optimistic: only 13% (6% + 7%) said there was only a small or no chance, and well over half the whole group, 57% (22% + 35%), thought there was a very good chance they'd have that college degree.

If you look at the answers for the subgroups defined by race/ethnicity or gender, most every group was pretty optimistic—only Hispanics had a little less than half saying their chance was very good. The women were a lot more optimistic than the men, and blacks had a really high percentage saying they were certain they'd get that college degree.

The two panels of this table, then, tell us a couple things about the 1980s Cohort (who, you may recall, represent the 18 million people born 1980–1984): they vary a lot in the grades they got in high school, but, rather surprisingly, most of them at the age of 14 or so were optimistic about their prospects of getting a college education. We'll see below if that optimism is borne out by the record they've achieved over the subsequent years.

Table 2.4: Schooling Level of the 1980s Cohort

	Population	Whites	Blacks	Hispanics	Females	Males
Panel A: The Highest Educational Degree Earned by Age 20						
None	15.4%	12.0%	24.4%	23.4%	13.4%	17.3%
GED	6.7	6.7	7.6	5.9	5.7	7.6
High school diploma	76.4	79.6	67.3	69.2	79.1	73.8
Associate's degree	1.4	1.6	0.7	1.4	1.6	1.2
Bachelor's degree (BA, BS)	0.1	0.1	0.0	0.1	0.1	0.1
Panel B: The Highest Educational Degree Earned by Age 25						
None	10.0%	7.8%	15.0%	15.7%	9.2%	10.8%
GED	10.4	9.5	14.2	10.4	8.7	12.1
High school diploma	47.8	45.2	53.1	55.9	45.0	50.5
Associate's degree	6.3	6.7	4.8	5.8	7.1	5.6
Bachelor's degree (BA, BS)	23.5	28.3	11.9	11.6	27.4	19.7
Master's degree (MA, MS)	1.5	2.0	0.8	0.4	2.0	1.1
PhD, JD, MD, etc.	0.4	0.4	0.4	0.2	0.6	0.2

Source: The 1980s Cohort.

The next table, table 2.4, tells us how much schooling these groups actually had completed by age 20 (in panel A) and later, by age 25 (in panel B). The 1980s Cohort members are not all age 30 yet, so we can't know what the table will show by age 30. Panel A tells us that by age 20 about three-quarters of the whole cohort (76.4%) had earned their high school diploma. Of course, very few by that age had completed college (only 0.10%). You'll notice, however, that some 15.4% had not earned their high school diploma yet, and an additional 6.7% had completed their GED (high school equivalency certification) but had not gotten their high school diploma. Looking across the columns, you'll see that a higher percentage of whites had earned their high school diplomas than was the case for blacks or Hispanics, and more of the females had earned their high school diplomas by age 20 than had the males.

Panel B in table 2.4 tells us the same facts, but for five years later, when the 1980s Cohort was age 25. By then nearly one-quarter (23.5%) had earned a four-year BA or BS degree, although blacks and Hispanics did not have nearly so high a percentage with a college degree.

So what have we learned about the schooling choices of the U.S. population born in the early 1980s? We see that they are pretty different from each other in how much education they got by their mid-twenties. More than 25% got a bachelor's degree or higher, but another 20% did not have a high school diploma. There are big differences both in how much education females got versus males (females got more), and whites compared to either blacks or Hispanics.

There's another important thing we can see from these data. If we look at the high school GPAs in table 2.3 and ask if these men and women were realistic about their prospects in education, the answer is seen in table 2.5. In this table, everyone is grouped according to their GPA, and we looked to see what each group said when they were 14 years old or so about their likelihood of getting a college degree by age 30.

We've also looked to see how much schooling they had actually acquired by the time they were ages 24 to 29. What we see is revealing: with each increase in high school GPA, their estimate of whether or not a college degree was likely rose pretty substantially. For example, those who had less than a C average in high school said the likelihood of getting a college degree was only a little better than fifty-fifty (53%), while those with a solid C said it was 66%, and right on up the ladder. Those with a 4.0 (all A's) assessed their chances at a very high 92%.

So one thing we see in the left-hand column of table 2.5 is that there is some reality in these young people's assessments—they knew their high school grades would affect their chance of graduating from college. But across the board many were overly optimistic about getting that college degree! Most everyone seemed to think it was a lot more likely than it really was. At the time of writing, these people aren't yet 30, so maybe many more of them will get a degree in the next few years, but we can tell from table 2.5 that those probabilities they thought were reasonable are higher than is the reality when they were 24 to 29 years old. For example, the B students (those with a GPA of 3.0) said, on average, that the likelihood of getting a college degree by age 30 was 78%. Table 2.5 tells us that only 28.3% of them—less than 3 out of 10—have that degree, and almost 1 out of 10 of them don't have a high school diploma (yet).

For even the all-A students, only two-thirds have earned that BA degree so far. Maybe optimism and a can-do attitude is a good thing,

Table 2.5: The Relationship between High School Grades and College Expectation and Attainment

High School GPA	Expectation of a College Degree by Age 30	Actual Percentage by 2009 (ages 24–29) with High School Diploma	Actual Percentage by 2009 (ages 24–29) with College Degree
< 2.0 (below C average)	53%	33.7%	1.4%
2.0 (C average)	66	67.5	6.2
2.1–2.9 (B to C average)	69	77.5	11.5
3.0 (B average)	78	90.9	28.3
3.1–3.9 (A to B average)	82	93.0	39.0
4.0 (all A's)	92	97.1	67.9

Source: The 1980s Cohort.

but you should remember this evidence when you assess your own chances of getting a college degree. Be realistic. (To be fair, these people were only ages 14 to 17 when they made their assessments, so you might be a lot more realistic now if you are already older than that.)

Looking at table 2.5, we can see that there is a really strong relationship between high school grades and graduation from both high school and college. The higher the person's GPA, the more likely he or she graduated from high school and from college. Now, we can't say from just seeing this relationship that the grades are actually the reason for, or the *cause*, of the different graduation rates. However, a lot of good research offers convincing evidence that grades do in fact have a strong influence on graduation rates. This is an application of that idea of putty and clay—early on in school, the decision about how hard you study and what grades you earn seems pretty much in your control, pretty malleable. But over time, as the years pass, the choices about doing or not doing homework made in earlier years influence how hard or easy it is to do well later in school; things get less malleable. The choices made earlier influence the opportunities available later. Table 2.5 tells us that this worked out in this way for the 1980s Cohort. That can be a sobering fact, but it is also highly motivating.

The next table (the last one for this chapter) also shows some pretty strong linkages, but it isn't so clear there that any one factor is the reason why, or the key influence on, the other factor. Table 2.6

Table 2.6: Relationship between Family Background and Completion of a College Degree by 2009

	Population	Whites	Blacks	Hispanics	Females	Males
Panel A: Father's Years of Schooling and Percentage with a College Degree or More						
< 12 years	7%	8%	6%	6%	10%	5%
12 years	19	21	12	16	25	12
13–15 years	30	32	26	18	35	26
16+ years	54	57	33	32	60	49
Panel B: Family Income Level at Ages 12–16 and Percentage with a College Degree or More						
< $20,000	7%	10%	5%	5%	10%	5%
$20,000–50,000	19	21	15	13	24	14
$50,000+	41	43	31	24	48	35
Panel C: Mother's Marital History and Percentage with a College Degree or More						
Ever Married	27%	31%	16%	13%	32%	22%
Never Married	8	12	6	9	11	6
Panel D: Region of Residence (1997) and Percentage with a College Degree or More						
Northeast	31%	37%	10%	13%	36%	26%
North Central	28	33	9	10	34	23
South	22	27	15	11	25	18
West	23	28	17	13	29	18

Source: The 1980s Cohort.

shows the link between several separate family background characteristics of the 1980s Cohort and whether or not they graduated from college.

Look first at panel A. You'll see that for every group (every column), the more education a person's father had, the more likely it is that he or she has graduated from college. The relationship is very strong: overall, of those whose father didn't have 12 years of schooling, only 7% have graduated from college; but of those whose father did have 12 years of schooling, 19% graduated from college. Of those whose father had some college, an even higher percentage, 30%, graduated from college, and, finally, of those whose father graduated from college or had even more schooling, some 54% themselves also graduated from college. Clearly, those whose father had more education also got more education themselves—that's a fact. Now, what should you make of that fact?

For one thing, this does not mean that the father's education caused his child to go to college—the fact of the relationship doesn't prove that the one thing caused or even had a big influence on the other. (Just because the relationship is really strong between your carrying an umbrella in the morning and it raining at noon that day, that doesn't mean that you "caused" it to rain!) You may have heard it said this way: "correlation doesn't imply causation," and that's the first point here.

On the other hand, we discussed earlier that parents' education is typically linked with the ability to pay for college, so in this case there probably is a real influence from father's education to the college attendance of his son or daughter. This correlation in table 2.6 doesn't prove it, but there's a lot of other evidence that convinces us.

The second point is that even if the relationship is "causal," there's a lot of room here for many other factors such as choice, motivation, and effort. Among those whose father didn't complete high school, 7% have already graduated from college. For the females, it was 1 in 10 who have done so. At the other end of the spectrum, among those whose father himself graduated from college, only 54% of the cohort have done so, thus far.

So even if it is the case that a father's education has a big role to play in a child's schooling attainment, there's lots of room for other factors. People have a choice—it's not predetermined. What you do and what you choose matters—and it matters a lot, whatever your father's schooling level.

The same point can be made for each of the separate panels in table 2.6. Panel B shows that there's a strong relationship between a family's income level when children were 12 to 16 years old and whether or not they had earned a college degree by their late twenties: only 7% of those whose family income was under $20,000 completed college, while 41% of those whose family income was more than $50,000 did so. So, panels A and B give us factual evidence that the economic circumstances of the cohort members when they were young were strongly related to their attainment of a college degree.

Panel C shows us something rather different: those people whose mother was married (including those who had been divorced or widowed) were a lot more likely to graduate from college than those whose mother had never married. That pattern, like most of the relationships in table 2.6, holds true for whites, blacks, Hispanics, and females and males, every group, big-time. Again, here this relationship does not mean that a mother being married actually caused her child to be more likely to graduate college. There can be lots of other factors that are related to her marital history and to the child's chances of graduating, factors such as the family's income, the number of kids in the family, the location in town where they lived that affected the quality of the elementary school and high school attended, or a lot of other things. And, again, what the table shows us is a fact, a relationship—not a destiny, not a certainty, not even a causal connection, for sure. It is useful and interesting to know, but it doesn't mean that there's no choice to be made.

One final point you might consider, however. These strong relationships between family background characteristics—such as father's schooling level (or mother's schooling level, which is just as strongly associated but not shown in these tables) or family income or the marital status of the parents—do show us that family background is strongly linked to college graduation of the kids. We can't say just why that's so from these tables, but we can say they are pretty tightly linked for this 1980s group. So when you make your choice about how much schooling to get for yourself, you should remember that there's strong evidence that your level of schooling is going to be linked to the level of schooling of your children. Your choice matters to you (and in the next few chapters, we'll detail some of the reasons it matters for your own well-being), and it is linked to your children's schooling levels years later. Again that's a reason why these are really life decisions; they have important consequences for you and for your loved ones, including those you'll love in the future.

Just so you don't think that everything in one's background is strongly linked to whether or not one gets a college degree, look at panel D of table 2.6. While there are some variations across the geographic regions in the United States, there isn't a strong consistent relationship here. Growing up in any of the four regions isn't tightly linked to whether or not a person later earned a college degree, and that's the case overall and for each of the three race/ethnic groups and for both males and females.

MORE SCHOOLING?

In this chapter we've considered an important life decision. We have introduced several concepts that can help clarify issues related to the choice about how much schooling to go after. We've discussed how the price reflects the costs and the values of the product, and how the price in this instance involves a lot more than money, since your time is an important "cost" element as you pursue your schooling. We've explored the trade-off of having something you want in the present or choosing to wait and have more in the future—your time preference. Waiting is more attractive the bigger the payoff, and that's reflected in the return on the investment in your "human capital."

We have considered some of the uncertainty surrounding a choice about more schooling and identified three general strategies for dealing with that uncertainty. We've talked about inequality in talents and in resources, and we've noted how schooling is a key vehicle to prepare yourself with the skills you'll need to climb higher up the rungs of the income ladder. While we've discussed these choices with a focus on college, the same issues arise for those considering whether or not to complete their high school education, to get some vocational training, or to go beyond college for a postgraduate professional degree. Your abilities, resources, interests, and many other circumstances enter into these decisions. The choice about schooling reflects that notion of putty and clay, since choices you make at one age have effects later—either opening doors for you or shutting down some options. That's one reason your time preference is so important: your future opportunities are tied to the choices you make today.

In addition to exploring these concepts, we've looked at a few relevant facts that can also inform your choice. Some of those facts come from government statistics about the whole society, such as the information in tables 2.1 and 2.2 that shows how the level of schooling is dramatically linked to higher earnings and to lower risks of unemployment. So that "return" on an investment in schooling has been, still is, and likely will continue to be attractively high. Yet no one level of schooling is the "right" answer for everyone. It depends on your interests, capability, access to funding, time preference, and much more.

For another set of relevant facts, we've begun to get acquainted with the choices made by the 1980s Cohort, those 18 million people born in the interval from 1980 through 1984. We've seen the wide range of their choices about their schooling and a few of the consequences. For example, we noted that in their early adolescence, most of them had high expectations about getting a college degree before they turned age 30, but for many that expectation was not met, at least not yet. This suggests that you'll want to be as realistic as you can be about your own prospects for subsequent schooling. For instance, when you are considering taking out a big loan to cover the financial costs of your schooling, be realistic and get as much information as you can about your prospects. Another fact we saw reflected in table 2.5 was how the 1980s group member's high school grades were linked to the level of schooling they subsequently achieved.

Concepts can guide you in making your choices. Facts can inform you about choices that others have made and how they've played out. A healthy dose of "reality" of what is (instead of what we'd like it to be) should be on the table when important decisions are being made. So we've made some progress. Let's move on in the next chapter to another important decision—what kind of occupation you think you might want to pursue.

THREE | Deciding on an Occupation

*Destiny knocks at the door of everyone at least once in a
lifetime. But in that moment, you have to be ready to answer.*
RICCARDO MUTI, DIRECTOR, CHICAGO SYMPHONY ORCHESTRA

Some questions you'll hear throughout your life are "What do you
want to be when you grow up?" or an age-appropriate "What line of
work are you in?" or just "What do you do?" One of the most common and convenient ways in which we often define ourselves as
adults is by responding, "Oh, I'm a lawyer" or "I'm a teacher." For
many people, their job is a big part of their identity.

You might think, "Why is it necessary to have a job? Maybe I'll just
skip that." But there are a couple pretty serious problems with deciding not to have a job or a career. You'll need income to live on over
your lifetime. For most of us, the income we get comes from working
at a job. Then, too, in some way you'll want to make your mark, to
have some influence on the world around you. One of the best ways
to do that is to find a job, a vocation, an outlet for your talents and
energy that allows you to make your contribution. Now, for a lucky
few, the income may already be there, thanks to a successful parent or ancestor, but you'll still want to have your own impact on the
world. You can surely do that without having a job. There are many
valuable contributions to be made in ways that don't involve a job
with a wage rate or a salary. Still, for nearly all of us, a job is both a ne-
cessity and one of the best ways to try to make the world a little better
place. So choosing an occupation is a big deal.

Since you might be in your occupation for most of your life, it's
pretty important that you choose one that you'll enjoy. You'll want
one in which you find pleasure in its challenges, that offers a good
outlet for your talents, and that gives you satisfaction.

Finding an occupation like that is difficult. For one thing, it's hard to know what is really involved in most occupations. How many different jobs do you know well enough to describe what a person does on a typical Wednesday morning? How does a banker start her day? What does a coder need to get done before lunchtime?

Some jobs are pretty routine, and you may know a little about them. But even for careers like teacher or dentist or flight attendant, where you've likely interacted with people doing them, you only see one aspect of what goes on, not all the stuff they do to get ready to teach or fix your tooth or give safety instructions on an airplane. How can you make a sensible choice about an occupation if you don't know what the job involves? That's just one issue.

Here are some others: If you think you might like to be a pilot, politician, or architect, how do you figure out how to do it well? How do you figure out what job really fits well with your interests? If you enjoy cooking, does that mean you should consider becoming a chef? What should you do this year to prepare? If you like to write, should you consider becoming a journalist, a novelist, or an editor? If you like to cook and to write, should you become a food critic?

And we haven't mentioned the earnings, which are one of the main reasons people get a job. If you enjoy playing basketball, you've probably noticed that some people make an amazing living doing just that. However, you're probably not that good or that tall, so a career in basketball may not be a realistic alternative—but then maybe you are the one for whom it is a real possibility. You've probably heard that you should work at something you really love to do and maybe that's basketball, for sure. What to do?

There are a lot of elements to a choice about a career or a job. Let's organize our thoughts and focus on what job to pursue, not how to get it. We'll begin with a little reflection on what a job is and why it is so important to you as an individual and to society at large.

PRODUCTION

People need and want a lot of things: food, clothing, housing, health care, transportation; also entertainment, information, advice, and many other goods and services. So many years ago, people did for themselves most of the tasks that met their needs—most people were a "jack of all trades."

But then people began to specialize a bit, and everything became much easier. Each person did one or a few things well, and then traded with their neighbors, who did some other tasks well, rather than everyone doing many things separately for themselves. Specialization in production, together with trade and commerce, led to a much higher standard of living and a better life for most everyone. It allowed for "economies of scale," where larger quantities of things could be produced at lower cost.

Several important things resulted from this, and most of them are attractive. Since a worker could produce more in an hour when he specialized, the value of his work rose, so his earnings did, too. That's the main advantage of the specialization we have today. Then, since the worker needed to trade his product for a lot of others to end up with the goods and services he needed, money—a general medium of exchange—was what he received for his labor services. He didn't need to trade his goods for the other person's goods directly, and that made the exchanges he wanted to make much easier.

But specialization also meant that we all became interdependent, relying on one another to make everything each of us wanted. By now we are no longer capable of providing all that we need for ourselves. Instead, we each make a contribution to the whole by our more specialized efforts, our "work." We are compensated with money that we can use to buy the products we need. This is the way our economy is organized, and while there are lots of choices you have, and much flexibility in just what you choose to do to earn your living, the nature of how jobs themselves are organized isn't one of the things you get to choose. There is a reality out there, and you will want to understand it and work within its constraints. Since specialization and large-scale production are part of that reality, you'll need to make a choice about what sort of job you'll want, and then what you can do to prepare for it.

The basic principle today is the same as in ancient days—you put in some effort and you produce something of value. What you produce helps meet the needs of somebody or their family. We are long past the era, if it ever really existed, when the fruits and berries, wildlife and fish of the lakes provided all that one needed for a full life without much effort expended beyond gathering them from the land.[1]

What happens today has been happening for generations: adults get up, go to work, and produce something of value for themselves or for others. So, that question, "What do you want to be when you grow up," is a respectful one. It means that the person asking it expects you to want to make a contribution to society using the skills and energy you bring to your job. That's how you play your role as a productive adult.

THE JOB AND YOU—FINDING A GOOD MATCH

The specialization of skills and the organization of production into large units offer society terrific benefits in terms of greater production. That's what has given us our higher levels of income. But this system means that we all have to make a choice about how each of us will make our contribution. How do you fit in? What tasks will you take on? What skills and efforts will you bring to the "labor market," where folks offer to work in exchange for money earnings?

Maybe the best way to think about choosing a job is to think of it as making a match. The challenge for you is to find a good match between the bundle of things you offer an employer and the bundle of things you want in exchange. That's the same challenge the employer faces: she's looking for a good match between the bundle of attributes of a worker—the skills needed to use the tools and work well with her other employees to produce her product—and the bundle of wages and benefits she can provide in exchange.

The challenge for both you and your ideal employer is to communicate what you each have to offer and to be clear about what you want in exchange. This show-and-tell is what the labor market is all about: offering what you have and finding the job that makes a good match for you and an employer.

YOUR BUNDLES—WHAT YOU SEEK AND WHAT YOU OFFER

Let's consider what you want to get from your job and then the bundle that you can offer in exchange. A successful job search, or a successful choice about an occupation, involves aligning those two bundles.

There are several things you'll probably want from your job. Money may be really important (and the more the better), but there are other things. You'll probably want to have some fringe benefits such as health insurance. You may be looking for some other perks from the job, like a pension program that accumulates savings for your eventual retirement, or the use of a company car, or sick time off with pay, or more.

And there are many other more general aspects of the job to consider. You may want a job that leads to even better jobs over time, as you acquire more skills and wider experience. You also may value the opportunity to learn on the job and to take on new tasks that keep you challenged. You will probably want to work with a supervisor who helps you get better at your job. Also, you will want a job that connects in some way with your own interests, that takes advantage of your skills. In general, there's value in a work environment that's pleasant and safe. If that isn't provided, you may not be productive and you may not be happy for very long. And after you've thought about just what you want your broader contribution to the world to be, you'll want to weigh the job in terms of whether it is going to help you reach that goal.

Now, you aren't likely to get everything on your wish list. And your prospective employer won't get from you all that she wants. It's important to give some thought to what you want and make some choices about what you value the most. Sometimes an employer can give you one thing instead of a couple others that really don't matter as much to you. Maybe, because of family obligations, you really value flexible work hours, for example. Some jobs can easily accommodate flexibility on when or where you put in your work hours, but other jobs cannot.

Turning to that other bundle, what you can offer to an employer, it will surely include your skills and knowledge, but also, importantly, your personal attributes like dependability, integrity, ability to work well with others and to communicate effectively, and, of course, your willingness to work hard.

We've talked about why specialization is useful and how it implies that each of us must make some choices about what to specialize in. We've said it is good to specialize in something you really like, because if you are lucky you may be using some of the skills you develop in your career for your whole work life. But there's an equally powerful element other than your preference to consider, and that is called your *comparative advantage*. Let's consider that for a moment.

When you think about yourself and your friends, you all have different talents. Some of you have greater athletic ability, can carry a tune, or tell a joke, or some of you have a better memory, are better at carrying on a conversation with someone you've just met, can make or keep friends more easily, are more attractive, or something else.

Now, it is possible that you have among your network of friends someone who seems to be better than you at everything, or almost everything. Lucky him! But that's less important, really, than something else: there are some aspects in which you are relatively better than most of your friends—even if by some absolute measure you aren't as good as a few of them are.

You'll want to think about and identify those characteristics or talents in which you are relatively good compared to other people (a good mentor can help you). Those personal attributes are the ones to build on, the ones to give a big weight in your thinking about a career. They are your comparative advantage, and that's what counts.

The principle here is pretty simple. Maybe you've heard that it's best for a country with lots of natural resources, like minerals or oil, to trade with countries that have lots of different resources, like labor or machinery or something different from what they have. The reason is that the gains from trading are greater for both countries if each trades with another that is quite different from itself in its labor or capital or raw materials.

The same principle applies to you: "the gains from trade"—the gains to you from offering your efforts on the job in exchange for the benefits you get—are greatest when you use the attributes that you have in relative abundance compared to other workers. So you'll want to consider what your comparative advantages are, build your skills to make good use of them, and offer them as part of the bundle you provide in your job. The nice thing about comparative advantage is that everyone has some!

Let's illustrate why your comparative advantage is so important. Consider a famous actress like Meryl Streep. She is an incredibly talented person and probably has a large home that needs cleaning each week. Now, maybe she's better at cleaning her home than a professional cleaner—she knows it well, she has energy, and she is just awesome, so let's suppose she can clean her home in two hours.

A nice guy on the other side of town runs a cleaning service and can also clean her house quite well, but it takes him five hours to do it. In terms of the time it takes, and assuming they both clean it equally well, Meryl Streep is clearly more efficient at cleaning her house. So you might think it's reasonable for her to clean her own house, since she's so much better at it than most anyone else.

But Ms. Streep's comparative advantage is in acting. The cleaning guy, while not as efficient as she is, has a comparative advantage in cleaning. Let's explore this, by considering what each could produce with the time it takes to clean her home if they did the next most productive thing they could do with that time.

In the two hours it would take her to clean her house, Ms. Streep might be able to give an interview about her upcoming new movie. The additional income that might net her from ticket sales could be a cool $10,000. So for her, while she's awfully efficient at cleaning, the opportunity cost for her in those two hours is really high.

For the cleaning guy, if he weren't cleaning a home with the five hours it would take him, maybe he would be driving a taxi. That would net him about maybe $35 an hour, for a total of $175. Not bad, but look at the outcome: if Meryl Streep cleans her house and he drives a taxi, in the time they spend, he gets $175 and she misses out on $10,000! So for both of them to be better off, even though it takes him a lot longer to clean her house, she can hire him and pay him more than $175 and less than $10,000.

That's the way with *comparative advantage*—the fact that she's absolutely better doesn't really matter, it's their relative skills that matter. When she or he or you use your talents in the activity at which you're relatively better, you and everyone involved are better off.

So don't worry about your friend who seems to be better than you at most everything. That's really rather irrelevant when you are considering a job or occupation. If you go with your comparative advantage and offer your services to the labor market based on those skills in which you are (or can become) relatively strong, you'll produce more at a lower opportunity cost, and you'll earn relatively more.

Of course, like nearly all the principles we talk about throughout this book, there are other considerations. It's possible that the occupation that most naturally uses your own comparative advantage has some other feature that just can't work well for you. So you'll need to consider alternatives, you'll want to weigh one thing and then another.

There aren't any simple formulas for what to choose, only some principles to guide you. Your values and preferences come into play in choosing your occupation as they do with other important choices you make. So, too, do your own capabilities, which are reflected in your comparative advantage and strengthened by your schooling and other training. There are other circumstances and aspirations you'll want to consider as you make your choice about your work career.

OPPORTUNITIES

So far the things we've noted for consideration when you make a decision about a job or career are things you learn about by *looking inward*, thinking about yourself. You'll see as we discuss other choices later that the same principle applies: first, look inward and know what's important to you—not what's important to your parents, your best friend, or to your mentor. These elements of the choice reflect your values and aspirations, your preferences and your capabilities. They help you know both what you want from your job and what you can offer in exchange.

After looking inward, it also makes a lot of sense to *look outward* at the jobs that might be available. There are several things to think about in this regard. It would be helpful to know more about what some jobs involve: What do they require in terms of know-how? What risks to your health or job security do they embody? How pleasant are they week in and week out? (Not all jobs are pleasant, of course, but if the pay compensates adequately for the yuckiness, the job may still be attractive.) How likely is it that these jobs will remain productive over several years? Do they involve a lot of travel, daily pressure, interactions with colleagues, learning opportunities, and the chance to make decisions on your own?

These or other attributes of a job may or may not matter to you personally. There are a lot of other dimensions of each job that matter to the employer, so they also can influence your choices. These include the knowledge needed to do a job well, the importance of good communication skills, quick thinking, physical strength, and so on. Some job requirements you can acquire through training or perhaps by practice and experience. Others you'll just not be able to get—for instance, your height might honestly rule out that attractive basketball career.

But another of the implications of all that specialization in the labor market is that there are an incredible number of fascinating little niches out there, jobs that require combinations of skills and know-how that one can't easily imagine in the abstract. The range of jobs is really incredible. But you can't get excited about a job you've never heard of or don't know exists, so it pays to look at the wide range of jobs at several levels of educational requirements and pay scales. You'll likely be amazed at what job opportunities are available if you put some effort into seeking them out.

Take a fellow I know, as an example: call him Fred. He is smart and learns things easily and has a good memory. He is shy and rather dull socially, a bit tedious but very orderly and methodical; he has some artistic inclinations but lacks much imagination. So, what sort of career might Fred pursue?

Well, first, Fred got well trained by earning a PhD in chemistry. He works in the chemical industry, writing and editing catalogs, describing and illustrating their products. He works from home most of the time and stays up-to-date on new inventions and materials so he can accurately describe them in the catalogs, and in fact he has become one of the leaders in his small niche industry.

Fred's career has been a big success, mostly because he found a job that uses his talents and doesn't require the skills he lacks, so the job match is quite good. He has exploited his comparative advantage. Consequently, with a lot of hard work along the way, Fred has had a very successful career.

PRESENT-FUTURE

There are several aspects of choosing an occupation that go beyond the issues we've considered so far. They make this choice particularly challenging but are worth some reflection. We'll consider three.

One of these is that your career choice involves that issue of the present and the future—your *time preference*.

There are probably jobs that would be attractive to you right now, jobs that you find appealing and don't require much knowledge beyond what you already have. You can probably compete successfully for one of those jobs now. But many of those jobs don't have a good prospect for the long run; they don't offer much room for advancement or career growth. Other jobs require stamina and youthfulness that you may have today but aren't likely to have in a few years. So selecting one of these occupations implies that you'll have to make a big adjustment in the years ahead.

These issues cause you to think about your time preference. Should you take one of those jobs available to you right now and have some income and get on with your life? Or does it make more sense to hold off, make some more investment in your skills, practice and build up your comparative strengths, and thereby make yourself more eligible for a job that has more long-run potential? There actually isn't a right or a wrong answer to that—what's right for you depends on your time preference.

Earnings typically rise over time with age, but the earnings in different occupations or at different education levels don't all show the same pattern. Looking at the fact of how earnings change with age can be informative. A key factor that distinguishes the pace of wage growth with age is the level of one's education. Table 3.1 shows that fact.

We can see several things in the pattern here. Looking from left to right, we see that as workers age, their earnings rise. They rise from the early twenties up until the early fifties, then fall off a bit. We can

Table 3.1: Annual Earnings Across the Lifetime, by Education Level
(in thousands of dollars)

Schooling Level	Age					
	21–24	25–34	35–44	45–54	55–64	65–74
All levels combined	$20.5	$30.2	$35.8	$38.1	$36.1	$28.3
Not high school grad	16.4	20.1	22.0	22.6	24.0	18.3
High school grad	19.6	25.5	29.4	30.3	29.9	23.2
Some college	20.7	29.0	35.2	36.9	36.3	29.1
Bachelor's degree	27.1	37.2	49.2	49.5	50.1	41.8
Advanced degree	27.3	43.1	58.9	59.2	60.4	56.0

Source: U.S. Census Bureau, "Table 1: Employment, Work Experience, and Earnings by Age and Education, Civilian Noninstitutionalized Population; U.S. both sexes," data from 2000 Census.

also see that earnings rise with age for all schooling levels, but notice how much faster they rise for those with more schooling. The rise from, say, ages 21–24 to ages 45–54 is $6,200 for those who didn't graduate from high school, but $22,400 for those who earned a bachelor's degree.

Here's where the present-future issue comes up: the differences by schooling level in earnings is substantial for people in their early twenties, but is much larger by the time they are in their forties. That is, the college graduate earns about 38% more than the high school graduate at ages 21–24, but by the time they are ages 45–54, the difference is a whopping 63%. Near term (now) the difference may not seem like it's all that large, but long term (later) it is. It's your choice, but make your choice knowing that these differences in salaries by schooling level rise as you age.

There's another element of an occupational choice that comes in here. At some point in your life—and now may be as good a time as any—you may ask yourself what you want to do in your lifetime to make the world a better place. It's not likely you'll discover a cure for cancer or solve our nation's need for new energy sources, but there is probably some big social issue or civic need, or a modest engineering breakthrough where you can make your mark.

You probably don't know now what it will be. But what you can spend some time thinking about now is what problem you'd like to address, what type of contribution seems most attractive and feasible for you. It could be something that might motivate or inform other people, something organizational that could make your community function better, or something mechanical that might develop into a product that makes life a little easier. It's not the specifics that matter at this stage; it's the broad character of what you like and what issues motivate you.

Almost no one at age 20 or so has a clear idea about what she will do in particular, so don't be discouraged by the fact that you don't know either. But then don't brush it aside just because you don't know now: make some choices about broad fields, think about those problems you'd like to help solve, and prepare and "be ready," as Maestro Muti says in the quotation at the beginning of the chapter.

You might enjoy looking at biographies of men and women who have been successful in the areas of interest to you. You'll typically find that they weren't that sure either when they were in their early twenties, but they did things to prepare for what might come up, and then they were receptive when the opportunity came along. That's true for most business leaders, great scientists, successful politicians, writers, you name it.

Let's note a case that's in a somewhat unusual career track, but a man who became one of the world's greatest twentieth-century contributors to our well-being. Dwight D. Eisenhower was born in 1890 in Texas, grew up in Abilene, Kansas, and went to West Point, having made the decision to pursue a military career.

Apparently he was only an average student in college but later excelled in the army's Command and General Staff School at Fort Leavenworth in his mid-thirties (there he was top of his class of 275). He worked under Douglas MacArthur in Washington, DC, and in the Philippines when he was in his forties, and when the United States entered World War II when he was in his fifties, he was both well trained and as experienced as an American soldier could be at that age.

He showed his skills in the battlefield and in the slippery world of military diplomacy, and he was asked to lead the Allies in what a great historian called "the largest most complex military operation in history," the D-Day invasion of continental Europe on June 6, 1944. He led the allies to victory in Europe and was later elected, twice, president of the United States. He helped end the Korean War and kept our country out of other wars for the duration of his presidency through the 1950s.

In his twenties soon after the end of World War I, Eisenhower could not have known just what his role would be in a military career. He seemed to know, however, that his comparative advantages included skills of leadership, strategy, vision, and persuasiveness (assisted by a smile that one of his generals said was worth twenty divisions of fighting men in any battle), and that these were well suited to a military life.[2]

So he got prepared, had the requisite skills and experiences, and when the call came, he delivered. You can do the same in your field. Maybe not at the grand scale of Dwight Eisenhower, but in your own way. So make some plans, select some areas in which you might excel. You never know when that call might come, but you can know that you intend to be ready when it does.

You'll see that when you think about an aspiration to do something really quite grand with your life down the road, the focus gives you useful direction for thinking about schooling and your occupation now. If a young Eisenhower knew that a military career was his aspiration, then going to West Point for college made a lot of sense. It did, in fact, help prepare him for the extraordinary task that he took on later in life.

One good way to get direction now is to focus on the product your life's work might generate. Another way is to explore not the outcome from your work but, instead, the activities along the way, the skills you'd like to develop because you enjoy them. If there's some particular bit of knowledge or piece of machinery, some type of animal or some language or culture that always intrigues you when you run into it, then work from there. Think what further you can do to pursue your interest in that topic. Consider what sort of career might make use of knowledge about that machine or might involve you working in that culture.

While the skills for many occupations come through formal schooling, there's also much to be said for the learning by doing that comes from having a job, doing it well, and moving from one on-the-job learning experience to another. A job working on a political campaign, for example, could turn into a position overseeing a small group in government service when your candidate wins office, and this can lead you to a career far from where you thought you'd be. The tasks undertaken in one job and the strategies and interpersonal skills you develop along the way can prepare you for bigger jobs. It is always a smart thing to see each job as a stepping-stone, one that gives you experience and connections that can help you move along in your career.

WHEN YOU'RE DONE WORKING

Before we leave this matter of present or future, there's another issue that you should give a little consideration, even though it will likely strike you as awfully distant and nearly irrelevant to you today. You will get old—if you're lucky. And if you do, you will almost certainly wish to retire and stop working week in and week out. But you won't want to stop eating, having a roof over head, or enjoying entertainment, so you'll need some income even if it doesn't come from continued earnings. Even though it's an awfully long time from now, let's make three quick points about preparing for your long-off retirement.

First, you are likely to live a lot longer than your grandparents! Even if you thought your older relatives were pretty ancient when you were a child, you have a good chance of living longer than them. Life expectancy—the number of years a person is likely to live—has been going up for a long time. Over the century from 1900 to 2000, U.S. life expectancy at birth grew from 47 years to 77. In a recent study based on data from 2008, life expectancy at age 65 was 18.7 more years overall (19.9 for females, 17.2 for males).[3] So when you turn 65 and might hope to retire, you'll still have 15 to 20 years of your life ahead of you, and you'll need food and housing every one of those years!

Second, compound interest is powerful. If you put $1,000 into savings for your retirement and do so at age 35, intending to retire at 65, you're giving that thousand dollars 30 years to grow. If it grows at a rate of, say, 4% each year, compounded (meaning the gain made one year is itself growing at that same rate in all the remaining years), at your retirement age it will be worth $3,243. It will have more than tripled. If you saved that $1,000 earlier—say, at age 25—by the time you retire at 65, its value will have risen to $4,801. That extra ten years of it sitting there growing at 4% added $1,558. During the first ten years, your $1,000 of savings only grew by $480, but in that fourth decade it grew by $1,558. That's why the compounding is so powerful: in that last, fourth, decade your savings was already larger, so it grew a lot more. Suppose you had made the savings at age 20 and you worked until age 70 before you retired and took it out to live on: over that 50-year period, your $1,000 would have grown to $7,107. So you should consider starting to save for your old age now, since every year you get some money put away earlier, its value will be larger when you are 60 or 70 or 80. (Can you figure out what the value will be at 65 of saving a larger amount at age 25?)

Third, you're not likely to be smart enough or lucky enough to do better than average with your savings—you're not likely to earn a rate of return higher than average. So most wise investment advisers suggest that you not put all your savings into any one company. Instead, put some where you can get it quickly if you have an emergency (e.g., in a bank savings account) and put most of what you save into a fund that matches "the market" (an index fund) and spreads your money among many investments. A really good book about your investments says, "Mutual fund companies are the way to go," and recommends a "no-load" fund with low fees since they are matching, not trying to beat, the whole market, so they typically cost less and generally do as well as other more expensive ones.[4]

RISKY BUSINESS

A second of those deeper issues that involve your career choice is risk.

You've probably played a few games of chance somewhere, maybe making a bet on a coin toss or scratching a lottery ticket. These are circumstances where there isn't really any skill involved. They are fun sometimes. Most of the risk you'll face in your career won't be this sort of pure chance, however.

Jobs are a little like financial assets. There are safer ones and riskier ones. In the finance world, a really safe way to hold your money is in a savings account at a bank. "Insured by the FDIC," your bank will emphasize, meaning that the U.S. government will give you back your savings even if the bank goes out of business. That's really safe. But the interest you earn on that very safe account tends to be low: investing with little or no risk is typically associated with a low return.

You could put your savings in another type of asset like a government bond or a corporate bond, and while the risk is a little higher, so too is the interest you'll be paid. Or you might put your money in corporate stocks. If you do that, you'll face a greater risk that you might lose some of your investment, but you'll also be compensated, on average, with a higher return. The likely higher return is the inducement to convince you to put your money into that riskier asset.

The same principle applies to your choice of an occupation: jobs that involve more risk tend to pay a higher wage. Some examples are obvious: a window washer who cleans only first-floor windows is paid less than one who washes windows hanging from a rope off skyscrapers. The risk and unpleasantness of sitting out there in the wind cleaning windows so high up is offset by a higher salary. That's true for jobs that involve other health risks like breathing foul air or being exposed to dangerous chemicals or life-threatening circumstances. Those jobs tend to pay a higher rate.

Another type of occupational risk is that some jobs won't last very long, so the pay needs to be higher to entice workers to take them on. One example would be a one-time task like building a dam on a particular river. Another example would be a job best done by someone of a particular age. That professional basketball career is one of these jobs—you just don't see 50-year-olds out there on the court no matter how good they were at 25. Basketball players have just a few years to make it in their career on the court, so the salaries are somewhat higher (among other reasons).

Let's go back to that risky investment and consider how that works out. Let's suppose you have a choice of one or the other of two investments. Investment A involves $1,000 and has no risk at all—it is a loan and you are certain to get your $1,000 back at the end of the year. We'll say A offers you a 5% return for the one year, so at the end of the year you will get $1,050 for certain. The other is investment B. It also involves investing your $1,000. With B you face a risk that one in ten times you'll lose half your investment, but the interest you'll be paid is 10%. So, with B you'll again *expect* to have $1,050 because you'll earn your $100 interest in all cases and in nine of ten cases you'll get your $1,000 back, but one in ten times, you'll only get $500 back: so you *expect* to have: $100. + 0.90(1,000) + 0.10(500) = $1,050. So if you were indifferent to risk, the two investments would be equally attractive to you. You would expect to get $1,050 from either one. Now, suppose there are 100 people who face these two choices, and 50 choose A and 50 choose B. At the end of the year, 50 people will have $1,050, 45 people will have $1,100 (those are ones who chose B and got their full investment back), and 5 people will have only $600 (those who chose B but then lost half their investment). So, while it was attractive to take the risk of B since the return was higher, some who did so ended up with less. That's the way a "risk" works—some will have good luck, but some will have bad luck. Risks bite! "Risk" means what it says: You might lose, and if so, you'll be less well-off; but if you don't lose, you'll be better off.

The same thing is true of jobs and occupations. Some who choose the riskier jobs earn a higher salary and do well. But others who choose the riskier jobs are unlucky, and they end up less well-off: some coal miners who breathe foul air in the mines contract lung diseases, some policemen get shot, and so on. Those who take the risk and have good luck end up better off than those who don't take the risk. But don't forget that some aren't so lucky.

Here, your preferences come into play again. Some people enjoy taking a risk while others are "risk averse," or don't like having the risk. Those latter folks will select investment A in the illustration above—they want to avoid the risk. Most folks are risk averse, but for many there is an amount of extra payment that can entice them to take the risk: if the extra payment is high enough. So, the question for you is just how risk averse are you? This, too, is one of your preferences that can and should influence your choice of an occupation—the greater your risk aversion, the less appealing is an occupation that involves considerable risk.

You shouldn't be discouraged from considering a risky option if it involves a "fair" risk, in the sense that the outcome you can realistically expect is as good as the sure thing. But don't think the higher return automatically makes a risky investment better—its higher return just neutralizes, or offsets, the risk. If you choose something risky, you might lose, but you might not—it's your choice.

There are many attractive features of taking risks. In lots of ways we all benefit from others' risk taking. Starting a new business is risky, for example, but if local entrepreneurs weren't willing to take risk, we'd never get a new restaurant or a new manufacturing plant in town. If skilled and curious men and women hadn't chosen careers in science that involved a lot of risk of failure, we'd not have many of the high-tech devices and conveniences we all enjoy today. The reason some folks are wealthy is that they took great risk and met with great success. And we all benefit from their success and probably should be appreciative of their vision, effort, and achievement.

This matter of risk should weigh on you a bit as you reflect on your own career choice. Taking a risk can leave you worse off or better off. You'll want to evaluate the likelihood of the good and bad outcomes realistically. Ask yourself how much the risk can be reduced by hard work or careful decisions along the way, and how much of it is really beyond your control. After you've considered these issues, you might still think it sensible to take the risk. Risk isn't always something you'll want to avoid—but neither is it something to take lightly.

ECONOMIC INEQUALITY

The third of these deeper issues involving your occupational choice is that of economic inequality. Since the bulk of most households' income comes from labor earnings, the difference in earnings across jobs is a primary determinant of the amount of income inequality in the nation.

Most of the inequality we see in how much money people earn reflects the fact that the value of their product from working varies greatly. The two major factors that influence that product are their abilities—both native abilities and acquired skills and know-how—and the effort they put forth. Some of the differences in earnings, of course, reflect the riskiness or other characteristic of the jobs undertaken as well as a host of other factors including sheer luck.

The way economic inequality may influence you is twofold. Most directly, the occupation you choose—including the efforts you make to be able to take on that job—has a major influence on your own earnings, and so that choice affects where you stand relative to others in terms of the level of your income. Higher earnings are, as we have discussed, one of the motivations for getting more schooling and more work experience, for taking a more risky or a less pleasant job, and for working more diligently and dependably. The combination of the many decisions you make about schooling, risk taking, personal habits, and so on have a big influence on the occupations that you can hope to get into. The resulting level of your income partly reflects those choices you've made. (There's that putty and clay again—choices that seemed pretty flexible at one stage in your life lead to less malleable circumstances a few years later.)

Similarly, since another important component of income is a return on savings, the choices you make about saving—how much and how you invest it—contributes to your income, especially as you get older and the savings accumulate (or don't).

Less directly, as you consider the choices you make about both savings and your schooling and an occupation that seems attractive to you, you realize that there are constraints on you, limitations on what your opportunities may be. You take these into account when you make your decisions. That's true of everyone else as well. Some of us are more fortunate than others in terms of all sorts of endowments and opportunities; some of us face far more serious constraints and demanding circumstances. What each of us can do is make reasonably good choices about the opportunities we have. Thereby, we can "make the most" of those opportunities and can justifiably feel pride in doing so. We can't choose those initial circumstances, but we see to it that we make sensible choices given the circumstances in which we find ourselves. We can also realize that this is true for others also: neither envy for those whose opportunities seem far better than ours nor scorn for those whose circumstances are less fortunate than ours makes much sense or does anyone much good.

SOME FACTS ABOUT OCCUPATIONAL EARNINGS

One of the reasons your occupational choice is such an important life choice is that it is the means by which your decisions about schooling and other forms of human capital are transformed into your contribution to society, the product from your work effort. Another reason is simply that you will likely be involved in your occupation for many years, and having one that offers you a good living and personal satisfaction is important. So it is useful to look at some facts about the linkage between occupations and earnings in the country. We'll do that, first, by considering some information about the whole U.S. economy and then by looking at how the folks in the 1980s Cohort are doing in terms of their earnings.

Overall, there were about 87 million full-time workers reported by the 2000 Census. They worked in about 500 different occupations. The median salary for full-year, full-time workers was $32,624. About 41% of them were females, and about 31% were college graduates. The median salary for the females was $27,888 and for the males it was $37,840.[5] (To put these salary figures in a little context, the official poverty level for a single person in the year these figures apply was $8,501, and for a household unit of two it was $10,869.)

Table 3.2 gives us more detailed information about the level of earnings in several occupations. It shows the median salary in the fifteen largest occupations in the United States (all those with more than 1 million workers) and in the five occupations with the highest and with the lowest median salary, based on the most recent government data. Reading the top row in panel A, we see that the biggest occupation—secretary—had 2,511,000 workers, that 12% of secretaries were college graduates, and that the median annual salary of secretaries that year was $27,000. It also shows the median salary for female and for male secretaries separately and tells us that 96.7% of all the secretaries were females.

There are lots of things we can see from this table. In interpreting the facts here, it is important to remember that the median salary is the salary of the person in the middle of the ranking and that the ranking includes those who have been working for many years and those who just recently began, those who are quite young and quite

Table 3.2: Occupational Earnings and Other Attributes (year-round, full-time workers)

Occupation	No. in Occupation (000)	Percentage College Graduates	Median Salary ($000)			Percentage of Occupation Female
			Population	Females	Males	
Panel A: The Fifteen Largest Occupations: Over 1 Million Full-Time Workers						
Secretary	2,511	12%	$27	$26	$32	96.7%
Teacher (elementary & middle school)	2,451	96	36	35	40	77.5
Truck driver	2,265	4	32	23	32	4.2
Sales manager	2,248	22	31	24	36	38.3
Manager (other)	1,662	50	52	41	60	32.6
Retail sales	1,567	21	27	21	32	39.4
Nurse	1,440	51	43	42	46	90.7
Accountant	1,370	72	42	36	51	54.3
Admin. support	1,398	25	33	31	41	66.0
Customer service	1,293	20	27	26	32	69.6
Supervisor/Mfg.	1,161	14	39	29	41	19.5
Sales rep/Mfg.	1,148	42	46	36	49	22.7
Bookkeeper	1,126	12	26	26	30	89.3
Janitor	1,066	4	22	17	24	22.7
Laborer/ materials mover	1,004	4	26	21	27	17.5
Panel B: The Five Highest-Earnings Occupations						
Physician/ surgeon	524	100%	$124	$87	$141	23.9%
Dentist	88	100	103	68	109	14.8
CEO	990	62	88	61	96	17.6
Podiatrist	8	100	83	52	90	12.3
Lawyer	708	100	82	67	91	26.0
Panel C: The Five Lowest-Earnings Occupations						
Teaching assistant	187	13%	$16	$15	$21	89.5%
Maid/ housekeeper	491	3	16	15	20	83.9
Café attendant	22	6	15	14	17	68.5
Child-care worker	487	11	15	14	22	95.5
Dishwasher	61	2	14	13	14	21.4

Source: U.S. Census Bureau, "Table 2: Earnings by Detailed Occupation, 1999."

elderly, those who work really hard and those who don't, those with a lot schooling and those who don't have so much, and so on. So interpreting these median salaries can be a bit challenging. That said, the table does tell us a lot.

Notice in panel B that a very high percentage of the people in those five highest-earning occupations have a college degree (the exception is the chief executive officers [CEOs] of companies). The percentage of those with a college degree in the lowest-paying occupations, by contrast, is quite low (see panel C). Schooling really does impact the earnings you can expect to get in your job.

There are a couple interesting facts related to gender. Look at how many of all these occupations have a percentage of females that is either higher than 80% or lower than 20%. Of the occupations listed, almost half of them do. Our occupations are highly gendered, either men's jobs or women's jobs.

You'll notice that in every occupation listed here—the biggest ones and the highest and lowest paying—the female median salary is lower than the male median salary. Some of these gender differences in salaries within an occupation are breathtaking.

A separate fact you'll see here when you compare the percentage females and the level of the occupation's earnings: the female percentage is quite low in those five highest-paid occupations, and it is really high in all but one of those lowest-paid occupations. "Female jobs" have lower earnings than "male jobs." And females in every one of these twenty-five jobs earn less than their male counterparts, on average. Maybe if you are looking for a purpose or cause to take up in your career, something worthy of your best efforts to improve the world, the pattern of earnings by gender seen here might motivate you.

Maybe. But before you express the outrage that this pattern might deserve, do recall that men have been working in lots of these occupations longer than women; that in decades past, men got a lot more schooling than women did; that men have typically worked more hours per week, more weeks per year, and so at any age have acquired more job experience. Those differences partly explains this gender difference in wages. Partly.

Let's pursue this issue one step further. There was an interesting recent study of the graduates from one well-known business school that looked at the earnings of male and female graduates over the subsequent ten years to see how their earnings compared and what might explain whatever gender differences emerged.[6] Since all these graduates had the same level of education and were about the same age and graduated at the same time—from 1990 to 2006—none of those factors could explain gender differences in earnings if there were any. And, in fact, the study reports that by nine years after completing their MBA (master's of business administration) degree, there were important gender differences in the earnings. Although the women and the men had "nearly identical labor incomes" at graduation, the study found big differences in their average earnings nine years later: the women's average earnings were $250,000 and the men's average earnings were $400,000 (in 2006 dollars). While both are very high levels of earnings (remember, all these men and women had earned an MBA), the men were doing a lot better than the women. Why?

The nice thing about this study is that the researchers could sort that out. What they found is that three factors explained most, but not all (some 85%), of the gender gap. The men had somewhat higher grades in their business school record and took more courses in the high-paying finance courses, and that explained about 25% of the gender gap. The men were less likely to have taken a period of time of six months or more without working during those nine years, and that explained just about 30% of the gender gap. Finally, men were working more hours per week than the women (averaging about 58 hours a week while the women were averaging about 52 hours per week, still a lot higher than the typical 40 hours), and that also explained about 30% of the gender gap. There was a substantial penalty in earnings of having taken several months off work for either the men or the women, but the women took those times off from work much more frequently and the reason seemed to be the presence of children. Career interruptions are costly in terms of continued growth in earnings, and women have those interruptions with greater frequency than men. That may have all kinds of benefits for her and her family, but it does suggest that much of the gender gap in earnings, at least among these highly educated men and women, reflects these family responsibilities that women, still, disproportionately take on. Remember, though, that in this one study, the researchers could only explain about 85% of that gender gap. There's still the other 15% that may be due to some sort of gender discrimination in the workplace.

Before we leave table 3.2, there is one other fact that just has to be noted. Among the five lowest-earning occupations in the United States, you'll see child-care workers. It seems we pay very little in our nation to those to whom we entrust the daily care of many of our children in their preschool years. We pay those workers on average just a little more than we pay those who wash our dishes. You might wonder why. It probably isn't because these are extremely pleasant jobs where the low pay is offset by the pleasure of working with children. It can be very hard work! It's more likely that one key reason is that this is a job that doesn't require a whole lot of formal education or training. Many states require child-care centers to be licensed and their staff typically must pass a background check, but the training requirement is typically low—some don't require a high school diploma while others require some courses in early childhood education, an exam, or a certificate. With relatively low requirements for certification, the supply of potential child-care workers is relatively great, and this keeps the wages pretty low. Then, too, if a parent is considering whether to stay at home and care for the child or go to work and put the child in some sort of child-care arrangement, the parent's own wage rate is an important factor in that decision: many can't afford to pay a lot more for an hour of child care than they earn, net, for their own hour at work. So both the supply of child-care workers is relatively high and the demand for child-care services is pretty sensitive to the price, which then impacts child-care workers' wage rates. All in all, then, it's a pretty depressing situation despite the fact that there are many wonderful and dedicated people who work hard at offering quality care for many of these children.

THE 1980S COHORT'S JOBS AND EARNINGS

Keeping in mind all the elements of a choice involved in choosing an occupation, let's see how those 18 million Americans born in 1980–

1984 are doing in terms of their jobs and their earnings by the time they were in their mid-twenties.

Before looking at the details, it is interesting to note that the 1980s group showed, even as teenagers, a pretty strong commitment to getting a job. They did so both by their actions and their expectations. We'll not have a table to show this, but the evidence is that between the ages of 14 and 19, about one-third of those in the 1980s group had worked for a total of more than 150 weeks (three years total), and another half of them had worked a total of 50 to 150 weeks (one or two years). The same is true for the cumulative hours they had worked from ages 14 to 19: some 21% of them had worked a total of more than 5,000 hours (that's more than two and a half years at full-time), and another 27% had worked between 3,000 and 5,000 hours in that six years. Only 5% of the whole 1980s group worked no weeks at all over that stage of their life.

We noted how many jobs seem to be "gendered" with a large percentage of males in that occupation or a large percentage of females. One pretty interesting fact about the jobs that the 1980s group had as young teenagers is how "gendered" those jobs were. Most jobs held by youths are casual odd jobs and not formal employment. They include a lot of babysitting, lawn mowing and leaf raking, elder care and child care, painting, delivery, waiting tables, and so forth. When those jobs are characterized as either "female jobs" or "male jobs" along the lines you'd expect, the fascinating thing is that some 84% of the jobs held by the females as young teenagers are ones that are pegged as "female jobs," and only 3% of the jobs held by females are ones pegged as "male jobs" (the other 13% hold jobs that are "neutral"). Similarly for the males, some 51% of their jobs are classed as "male jobs," and only 20% are "female jobs" (28% of the jobs held by the males are "neutral" ones). The pattern holds for whites, blacks, and Hispanics in the 1980s group.

It works just as strongly the other way around as well: a typical "female job" is babysitting, and 85% of the teens ages 12 to 15 who reported doing babysitting were females; lawn mowing is a typical "male job," and, sure enough, 94% of the teens 12 to 15 years old who reported doing that job were males. So even at a young age, the 1980s Cohort sorted themselves into jobs that have a gendered character to them. It may be attractive to think of jobs ideally as all neutral and as equally available to one as to the other gender, but much of the imbalance is the result of choices that workers themselves make, not barriers or restrictions in the job market.

Regarding their work expectations as well, when asked at the age of 14 or so, "What is the percent chance that you will be working for pay more than 20 hours per week when you turn 30?" more than half of the 1980s group answered "100 percent." So even as quite young kids, the men and women in the 1980s Cohort said they expected to have a job when they turned 30 and, indeed, by the time they reached age 20 they had already acquired a surprising amount of job experience. So, now then, how are they doing in terms of hours worked and earnings by age 25?

Table 3.3 tells us about that. Panel A shows the amount of work they were doing, while panels B and C tell us what their wage rate and annual earnings were. If you work full-time, that means you put in around 2,000 hours of work in a year. In panel A we see that almost half of the 1980s Cohort were working full-time when they were age 25 (33% were working 1,800–2,500 hours, and 15% were working more than 2,500 hours). We can also see that, overall, only 12% did not have employment at that age. For blacks that percentage was 18.

When we look at hourly wages (panel B) and total annual earnings (panel C) from all jobs at age 25, we see a rather sobering fact. While 14% have a wage rate that is $20 or more, 12% have a wage rate under $7 an hour. (Just for comparison, the U.S. minimum wage during these years of 2005–2009 ranged between $5.15 and $7.25. The U.S. official poverty threshold for a single person in that interval of time ranged from $9,973 in 2005 to $10,956 by 2009.)

You can clearly see here the considerable disparity in income that one reads about so often, and this was before the economy collapsed near the end of 2008 and many jobs were lost. (Since these men and women were born 1980–1984, they were age 25 in the years 2005–2009, so the information in table 3.3, on individuals when they were 25, is mostly from before the economic crisis.)

If we look in panel C at what percentage of the 1980s group had annual earnings under $5,000 and compare that to the percentage with annual earnings over $40,000, we see that there are just about

Table 3.3: Annual Hours Worked, Wage Rates, and Annual Earnings, at Age 25

	Population	Whites	Blacks	Hispanics	Females	Males
Panel A: Annual Hours Worked						
None	12%	11%	18%	12%	13%	12%
< 1,000	16	16	20	17	19	14
1,000–1,800	23	24	22	22	26	21
1,800–2,500 (full-time)	33	35	28	35	32	35
> 2,500	15	15	12	15	10	19
Panel B: Hourly Wage Rate						
< $1	1%	1%	2%	2%	1%	1%
$1–7	11	10	13	11	14	8
$7–12	40	38	53	41	42	39
$12–20	33	35	24	34	31	35
> $20	14	15	8	12	11	17
Panel C: Annual Earnings (total, all jobs)						
< $5,000	12%	10%	21%	12%	15%	9%
$5,000–20,000	35	34	38	35	39	32
$20,000–40,000	41	42	34	43	38	43
> $40,000	13	14	7	10	9	17

Source: The 1980s Cohort.

as many in the low category as in the high category. But across the three race/ethnic groups, there are big differences: for whites we see there are more in the high-end category; but for blacks there are three times as many in the low-end category, and for Hispanics a little more in the low end. Similarly, for females there are a lot more in the low end, and this pattern is reversed for the males.

There are lots of reasons for all this disparity among individuals, and lots of choices along the way that have been made that have affected this dispersion. But it is a fact that there is a lot of variation in what these 25-year-olds experience in terms of their earnings.

We've talked a lot about the link between education and earnings, so let's see if it is evident in the experience of the 1980s group. Table 3.4 investigates that. In panel A, the first row of numbers reports on those who had *not* earned a college degree by age 25. It shows that 15% of them had a wage rate less than $7, 46% of them had a wage rate between $7 and $12, 29% had a wage rate between $12 and $20, and the remaining 9% had a wage rate higher than $20 an hour. Compare that to the row immediately below. It reports on those who

Table 3.4: The Relationship between the 1980s Cohort's Schooling and Earnings at Age 25

Panel A: Having a College Degree and the Wage Rate at Age 25

Have College Degree?	Wage Rate			
	< $7	$7–12	$12–20	> $20
No	15%	46%	29%	9%
Yes	6	24	44	26

Panel B: Having a College Degree and Annual Earnings at Age 25

Have College Degree?	Annual Earnings at Age 25			
	< $5,000	$5,000–20,000	$20,000–40,000	> $40,000
No	13%	38%	39%	10%
Yes	8	27	44	21

Source: The 1980s Cohort.

did have a college degree by age 25. Many fewer (only 6%) of them had a wage rate no higher than $7, while a much larger percentage of them (26%) had a wage higher than $20. We see the same qualitative fact when we look at panel B at their annual earnings: those with a college degree have about half as many with earnings of $5,000 or less, and more than twice as many with earnings of $40,000 or more, compared to those without a college degree. So, indeed, yes! The relationship between schooling and earnings is seen very clearly in the experience of the 1980s Cohort by their mid-twenties. We can expect that relationship to get even stronger as they continue along their life course.

The next table shows the relationship between the 1980s Cohort's family background and earnings at age 25. You'll see tables like this from time to time, and generally the message that accompanies the table is that there's a destiny here, a nearly predetermined outcome. You'll see it argued that if you grew up having a lot, in a family that had a pretty high income and parental education, you will do well in life, and that if not, you will find life pretty difficult.

The table shows that there is, indeed, a moderately close link between the 25-year-old's earnings and his or her circumstance as a young adolescent. But there's another way to interpret the facts here as well. Let me show you.

Table 3.5: Family Background Characteristics and Education Level by Annual Earnings at Age 25

	Annual Earnings at Age 25			
	< $5,000	$5,000–20,000	$20,000–40,000	> $40,000
Percentage of the population	12%	35%	41%	13%
Panel A: Family Income When Age 14				
> $10,000	17%	10%	7%	6%
$10,000–50,000	51	51	46	36
> $50,000	32	39	47	58
Panel B: Father's Education Level				
< 12 years	27%	20%	16%	10%
12 years	34	37	38	32
13–15 years	16	20	21	23
16 years or more	23	24	25	34
Panel C: Family's Poverty Status When Age 14				
Poverty Status*				
In poverty	36%	24%	20%	12%
Slightly above poverty	27	30	28	25
> two times their poverty level	37	47	52	63
Panel D: Own Education				
No college degree	82%	78%	70%	55%
College degree	18	22	30	45

*Ratio of family income to family poverty threshold less than 1.0, between 1.0 and 2.0, or above 2.0, respectively.
Source: The 1980s Cohort.

Table 3.5 splits the 1980s Cohort into four groups, according to their earnings at age 25. Some 12% of them had annual earnings under $5,000 when they were age 25; they are all in the left-hand column of table 3.5. What we see as we look down that column in panel A is that many of them did grow up in families with low income—17% of them lived in a family whose income was less than $10,000—and only 32% grew up in families with income higher than $50,000.

The next column over includes only those with earnings at age 25 between $5,000 and $20,000, the third column includes those with $20,000 to $40,000 and the right-hand column includes those with earnings over $40,000. Only 6% of that high-income group grew up in a family with less than $10,000 income, and well over half (58%)

grew up in a well-off family. That's the sort of evidence that "those that have get" and "those that don't have don't get."

You'll see that same pattern in panel B, which shows their father's education level, and in panel C, which shows their family's poverty status when they were 14 years old. All three of these panels show a pretty strong connection between how the person was doing economically at age 25 and the economic circumstance in which he or she grew up.

But look at that table again with a different eye. Since the first three panels, A, B, and C, essentially show the same pattern, let's talk it through using panel C, the poverty status of the family. Of those who are doing quite well at 25—with earnings that year over $40,000—more than one in ten of them (12%) grew up in poverty. That is, one in ten of the most successful at 25 were among the least well-off living with their parents a decade before.

Look at the other end of the spectrum, those whose income was less than $5,000 the year they were 25. More than a third of them (37%) grew up in a pretty well-off family whose income exceeded their poverty level by a factor of more than two.

So there are many in the 1980s Cohort who are succeeding even though they grew up in economically deprived families. And there are many who are not (at least yet) succeeding economically who came from economically successful families. Something made a difference, and it's likely the choices the person himself or herself made along the way played a big role in that difference, either for the better or for the worse. So, yes, there's a strong link to family background, but no, it's not destiny: you have choices; you have influence—what you choose to do makes a big difference.

Another way to see this is to compare the pattern in panel D of table 3.5 with that of the previous panels. The one of the four panels that shows the strongest link with earnings at age 25 isn't the family background measured as family income at age 14 or father's education or the family's poverty status: it is the person's own education level. Family background surely matters, but the person's own choices matter greatly as well, and we might expect their own choices to have an even larger influence as they grow older.

No matter where you start out, your own choices affect your success. Nothing really insulates or effectively protects you, and nothing prevents you from moving up the ladder. Table 3.5, despite the dominant pattern it reveals, shows that your own decisions matter a lot.

YOUR OCCUPATION

Choosing a life's work, an occupation, is a big deal. In our technologically sophisticated world, it takes a pretty demanding understanding of math and science, as well as skills in communication, to play a productive role as a member of the labor force. In this chapter we've discussed why our country's production is so much greater when workers specialize and deepen their skills in a few tasks. But specialization requires choosing just what knowledge and skills you'll develop as your human capital.

We also talked about production and how your efforts on the job fit in and why it is that some jobs pay so much higher salaries than others. Some of our attention was focused on making a good match between what you want from a job and what various jobs offer you. Finding a good job for yourself is a real challenge because there are so many elements of the choice both from your point of view and that of your employer. One of the important issues is your comparative advantage, which you'll want to come to understand and make use of, and the good thing is each of us has some.

The issue of the present versus the future is important in choosing an occupation. We saw that the pattern of growth of earnings as you age differs a lot by schooling level. More schooling typically means a faster growth in earnings over your lifetime but a somewhat delayed start to your working life. So your time preference has an important role to play here. We noted that another present-or-future issue comes up when you think about saving for your retirement. We noted three things to consider: (1) You are quite likely to have a lot of years of life beyond, say, age 65, so you'll need more accumulated savings than you may think; (2) the sooner you put some money away for your retirement the better off you are, since compound interest assures us that savings will grow bigger the longer you allow it to grow; and (3) there are some pretty simple rules of thumb about sensible savings strategies, and they don't rely on your being wildly clever or lucky, so they are worth knowing and using.

We talked more extensively in this chapter about risk, how it works, and why it affects the levels of earnings among occupations and also how it plays out with some winners and, for sure, some losers. But that doesn't imply you would be foolish to take some risks in your job choices. Like the poet Robert Frost said, "Two roads diverged in a wood, and I—I took the one less traveled by, and that has made all the difference." But Mr. Frost didn't tell us just what difference it made; you'll get to find out for yourself when you've made your own occupational choice. Maybe you'll choose to be a poet also.

FOUR | Decisions about a Partner

Tennis is just a game. Family is forever.

SERENA WILLIAMS

One of the principal transitions from childhood to adulthood is moving from your parents' home to a home of your own. It is a rite of passage that can occur at an early age as a mid-teenager or much later. This is a transition fraught with uncertainty and hope, exciting prospects and bewildering choices. Like so many of the big decisions in life, this one is all tied up with other choices. The housing choice is only a small part of this bundle of decisions. Perhaps the most influential issue is when and how to shift your primary relationship from dependence on your parents to being fully responsible for yourself.

Young children are necessarily dependent on their adult caregivers for most everything from their nourishment and shelter to offering guidance about acceptable behavior, satisfying their boundless curiosity, and teaching them social skills like sharing. But at some stage a young person distances herself from that comforting parental oversight and financial support and begins to make her own decisions about how to earn a living, where to live, and with whom to live. In this chapter we'll focus on the choice about whether and with whom to partner. You'll also find that lots of the same issues arise in the choices about friendships, activities, and lifestyle.

It wouldn't be very effective if you sat down and tried to decide which of your friends you'd like to have as your life partner, for a whole lot of reasons. Most importantly, you probably don't know what you will want to be doing in your life in ten or fifteen years, so it's awfully difficult to imagine with whom you would like to be sharing it. You need to explore your own preferences and decide what's important to you, then you can build from that self-knowledge in making decisions about a partnership.

Also, like most everything in life, it takes some skill to be a good partner and to understand how to communicate and interact with someone as an equal. You'll want to bond tightly with your partner and share much, but at the same time retain your own identity and values. You'll benefit from practice here as in so many other areas. So having a best friend, a confidant, maybe a lover can help you know both yourself and how to be a good partner. Trying it out can also help you know what sort of partner you'd like to have. So it makes sense to take this life choice in stages.

Let's first consider *why* you might want to have a partner in your adult life or whether it is more appealing to you to live as a single person. After considering why, we'll think about *who* would be a good partner in the sense of what attributes and characteristics you hope to find. We'll think about whether you might prefer several short-term relationships or a long-term mate. Then we'll talk briefly about *how* to go about finding one. We'll consider the uncertainty surrounding the choice, as well as what is surely one of the reasons why you might want a partner—sex. We will consider this aspect explicitly below.

PRODUCTION

After you've completed your schooling and have found a job, for each week of most of your adult lifetime you'll likely spend around 40 hours at work and maybe an additional 10 hours getting there and back. If you spend a typical amount of time sleeping and in personal care and exercising, that will account for an additional 70 hours a week. That leaves you nearly 50 hours of time each week awake, at home or out doing something other than your full-time job.

One way to think about these 50-or-so hours is to imagine that you are a little business, buying materials that you use to manufacture the goods and services that you then consume and enjoy. For example, think about your meals. You have a kitchen full of equipment like a stove and pots and pans for making meals. You buy and bring in sacks full of raw material like fruits and vegetables, meats and spices. You use some know-how that your parents showed you or that you got from a cookbook or online. You use some manpower to cut up the veggies, season the salad, and produce your dinner, night after night. You are a little firm, producing the things you enjoy and consume, using capital, labor, and technology just like the local manufacturing plant does, only at a small scale and mostly for your own consumption, not for sale in the marketplace.

You can even think of the other hours of the week as contributing to the same end: your employment yields earnings so that you can afford to buy those groceries and the household capital equipment in your kitchen (and your garage and your living room). The sleep and personal care time also is necessary to keep your body in good condition for the laboring you'll do around the house.

Now, not all the time is spent cooking and cleaning. Some time (hopefully a lot) is spent hiking or reading a good book or going to movies or just hanging out or whatever your form of entertainment may be. That time, too, can be viewed as productive, using your own time and effort in connection with some purchased equipment (those hiking boots) or goods and services (a movie ticket or a personal trainer) to generate the products that give you a lot of pleasure. You are indeed the CEO and a key laborer in the productive enterprise that you and your friends know as your home life.

In chapter 3 we noted that one reason most of us don't make all our own products is that it is so much more efficient to coordinate with others. Those same economies of scale are one of the main reasons why you might want to have a live-in partner. Many of the issues involved in the choice about having a partner are similar to those we discussed about choosing a career. To think this through, set aside for now all the stuff about love and sex and babies (we'll come back to that) and consider what goes on in daily life, day in and day out.

You produce a lot of things that you then enjoy consuming, from dinner and a clean living room to going to a good movie. If you shared those activities with someone, both you and that other person might be able to produce a lot more together than the two of you could separately. Just like in a manufacturing firm or a hospital or the bank down the street, there are substantial economies of scale in household activities.

You may have heard the old adage that "two can live as cheaply as one." That's a bit of an exaggeration, but there has been a lot of

Table 4.1: The Magnitude of Scale Economy in Household Size*

Persons	Equivalent
1	1.00
2	1.62 ← (not really two as cheaply as one)
3	2.16
4	2.64
5	3.09 ← (5 live together about as cheaply as 3 separately)

*An equation that reflects these scale economies counts adults, A, and counts children under 18, K, and then uses the little formula, Scale = $(A + 0.7K)^{0.7}$. That yields the values seen in the table for adults. For a discussion, see C. F. Citro and R. T. Michael, eds., *Measuring Poverty: A New Approach* (Washington, DC: National Academy Press, 1994), p. 59.

research to figure out just how much advantage there is in the scale of operation in a household. Table 4.1 uses this research to estimate how close two people can actually come to living as cheaply as one person.

According to these estimates, when two people live together, instead of needing twice as much income for the two of them, they can live just as well with about 60% more than one person alone, not twice as much. And those economies of scale continue in larger households, as you can see. Why might that be so? The reasons are essentially the same as for the firm.

For one thing, a lot of costs are lower if you buy in bulk. Consider the cost of groceries. The cost per bowl of cereal is lower if you buy a large box, partly because the "fixed" costs—packaging, shipping, storing, marking, and scanning at the checkout counter—are about the same for the company that made the cereal and for your grocer whether you buy a small box or a large one. Once those fixed costs are paid, it doesn't cost so much more to sell larger and larger boxes of cereal. So the cost of providing you, the consumer, a bowl of cereal is lower if you buy a larger box.

This idea also works with the time it takes you to get those groceries. It takes almost as much time at the store to walk the aisles and pick up the stuff you need, to go through the checkout line, carry things home, and put them away, whether you are shopping for one person or for two or three or four. That time spent shopping is nearly a fixed amount, so the more people you're shopping for, the lower the time cost per person. That's true of a lot of the things you buy for both the money cost and the time cost. So living in a household with more than just yourself offers some big economic efficiencies. That's one reason people live in households with more than one adult.

And there are many other economies of scale. There's a lot of stuff you need in your home, but you don't need it exclusively or all the time. Things like a telephone or a shower or a dishwasher or a TV or a coffeemaker and much more. These are things that two can share and save a lot of money on by not having one of each for every person.

Another set of things around the house actually can serve several people all at once, without inconvenience or sacrifice by anyone. These are things like a security lock on the front door, an electric light in the room, or music from a radio. These are called "public goods" when they exist in your neighborhood and in our country— things like the beauty of the lake on the edge of town and the streetlights at night. An example of a public good at the country level is our strong national military defense, which protects us all without requiring that any of us forgo any personal protection to provide it to our neighbors also. In fact, for many of these public goods, we couldn't avoid sharing them even if we wanted to. That's also true of some of the public goods in your home.

For all these reasons, there are big gains to living with someone, sharing space and household equipment, so when you move away from home, you are likely to want to have a roommate. It's economical. But there's a pretty big difference between having a roommate and choosing a life partner. Much of the difference has to do with the time involved in the partnership and some coordination of who does what around home, so we'll leave that to a discussion below.

Those economies of scale are one big reason for choosing to have a partner. While that reason is economic in nature, another, quite different reason is psychological: for many, it is nice to have a companion. You probably grew up in a household with several people, and you may like having someone around after you move out of your childhood home. It is helpful to have someone to think through choices with you: What movie shall we see? How will we spend our Saturday? Should I go to the doctor about that rash? Should I buy that new thing, or save some money and put up with the old one for a while longer? It can be lonely unless you have a close friend to chat with, to plan with, to just hang out with, and it is surely more conve-nient if that friend lives with you than having to go out every time you want to be together.

Living together you can more easily build your relationship, come to know one another all the better, really get to share and feel close, comfortable, trustful, intimate, loving. People pair off for a reason— notice how many people walking down the streets of cities are couples or pairs—and for many it is really nice to have a truly close friend, and that person is most often a partner of some sort. So there are powerful psychological as well as economic reasons for choosing to have a partner.

Now, as with most of the choices we discuss throughout this book, that does not mean that you should have a partner or that you are making a mistake if you do not do so. There are good reasons for not having a live-in partner, and it is really a choice, not an obligation or a foregone conclusion that you will want one.

For one thing, a partner imposes constraints. If you greatly value independence of action, you may prefer to protect your free-spirited life alone without the burden of coordinating with anyone. If you can find the companionship you want from a friend who is a bit more distant, then you might choose not to have a partner. You'll give up some things by living alone, but you'll also gain some others, in-cluding a privacy you'll not have if you share your living space. It's a trade-off. Like I've said before and will say again, the choice is yours.

COORDINATING WITH YOUR PARTNER

Now let's move from why you might want to have a partner, to who might be a good partner. Not in the sense of choosing Pat or Alex, but in terms of the type of person that might be right for you. When we discussed choosing a career, we talked about how you will prob-ably do only one specific part of the production of whatever product your firm makes, and how others will do other parts of the work. By focusing on a smaller-than-the-whole project, you specialize and get better and better at doing a piece of the work. That can also be true with your roommate or partner: you and he or she can divvy up the work, specialize, and get more efficient at some tasks, since you won't have to do some other tasks that your partner can take on. There are lots of these sorts of chores in the home and dividing them up makes sense.

There are probably some of these tasks at which you are particularly good and some at which you aren't so great. Keeping the books and paying the bills? Tinkering with the electric circuits in the house and getting the wattage right for the new heater? Caring for the lawn? Caring for the car? Being the social secretary and keeping track of which nights you're seeing those friends? There are lots of little tasks, some of which you probably like doing and others you really aren't very good at. These are tasks that if both you and your partner did them, you would probably just get in each other's way. They are tasks you can do better alone than you can working jointly.

To take advantage of those economies of scale when it comes to splitting up these tasks and coordinating your activities, it starts to matter who that partner is—not every potential partner is equally attractive from this point of view. If you could find just the right partner, you'd get one who is good at doing the things you don't like doing, or aren't good at, and then you'd trade or share—you doing the tasks he doesn't like or isn't good at, and him doing the ones you don't like.

There's yet another principle that comes into play here. The tasks we just talked about are ones either one of you might do alone. But there's another set of activities that you'll want to work on together. These are activities where you'll share time and "produce" your product jointly—and there are a lot of them. They include having a good conversation or a great discussion about the implication of the movie you saw last night, or making a barbeque dinner, or making love, or the hour on the tennis court together. These "productive" activities aren't ones you'll want to turn over to one of the two of you! The two of you will want to do them together.

In fact, some of the most important activities you'll undertake in your household are ones you'll want to coordinate and complete together. These include, for example, decisions about big financial events like buying a house and behaviors related to your religious beliefs. These are activities in which you and your partner will work together, and it will be important that you share those interests and values. Another very important shared task is raising children. It's a lot easier if you have similar aspirations for your kids and have generally the same philosophy about raising them. Less important, if your partner loves to go dancing but you prefer to watch sports events, you'll not complement one another as well as you would if the two of you both preferred the same thing.

Now, then, you may have noticed that there are two quite different issues at work here in the reasons why one person might be a better partner for you than someone else. In the tasks that one of you can do just fine, it's best to find a partner who doesn't share your talents, so you and she can coordinate by one of you doing one job and the other of you doing another. You *substitute* for each other here and, in terms of these tasks, the more different you are, the better off you both are. In effect, you produce separate things you both want and then you trade. It's a little like the trading that goes on in the international marketplace for goods and services: as we discussed earlier, the gains from trade are greater the more different the trading partners are. That applies to you and your partner as well.

On the other hand, the other set of activities are ones where you and your partner work together, and each enhances the value of the effort of the other, where you *complement* one another. This distinction between substituting or complementing one another is found in all sorts of production. For instance, some machines substitute for human effort (e.g., a robot), while others complement it (e.g., a computer). Substitutes replace your efforts and working with it actually lowers your own productivity; working with a complement makes you more productive.

So, does this all imply you're better off looking for a partner who is the most different or the most similar? It turns out that by far the more important set of activities in most households are the ones that depend on you and your partner being complementary—raising the children, tending your spiritual needs, sharing and enjoying time together. So it is probably wiser to look for a partner who is similar to you in the ways the two of you share time and effort and value similar outcomes. Only secondarily it is also good strategy to find a partner who can do some of those substitutable tasks for you and who is glad to have you do some of the other ones.

Then, too, there's yet another consideration and that has to do with how long you think this partnership will last: is this a roommate for the year, or a partner for several years, or maybe a life partner or spouse from now until "death do us part"? Once again, this is an important issue that involves the present and the future.

PRESENT-FUTURE

We confronted the issue of the present and the future in both the decisions we've discussed so far, schooling and careers. In thinking about choosing a partner, this concept is important in a different way. In those previous choices it was a matter of making an investment, incurring costs now, and preparing for something down the road that would work out better because of that investment. That's not the issue in the choice of a partner.

To show how the idea of present-future does come in handy here, a few examples can help clarify. Let's imagine your partner loves to spend time at the beach, but you're not all that interested in it. It may still make sense to try to find some things to do at the beach so the two of you can share the time together. That's true of the sort of movies you enjoy and many other things. If you have some pretty specific common interests and activities, you'll have a better time together. But to develop them takes time, planning, a commitment to staying together, and some coordinated strategies.

That's all the more relevant when it comes to important issues like how to raise children, what religious affiliation you may choose, even the very principles that will guide your behavior. In these big areas, it matters a lot that you have a compatible partner, one who shares your values and preferences. We've stressed that you'll want to give this some thought as you search for and select a partner. It is just as true that after you've gotten together, you'll both want to plan together how you'll pursue those common aims.

Maybe you know couples who, after they got together, planned a strategy of both getting more schooling, one at a time while the other got a job and supported them both. That can lead to two good jobs in the family when the training is all complete. Getting the education both partners want is just one example. Choosing complementary careers that don't have the same risks from an economic downturn is another. Both partners investing emotionally, wholeheartedly, in the kids when they come along is yet another. If you and your partner are thinking long-term and planning in a coordinated way, these strategies pay off big-time.

There's a downside to this, however. If you and your partner make these joint plans and commitments, about children or schooling or careers, and then your partnership comes to an end abruptly or unexpectedly, that can be a really big setback for both of you. That's why this issue of thinking about the present and the future is so important in terms of longer-term partnerships.

All that jointly generated activity that makes so much sense when you were together doesn't have nearly as much value if you split up. This is also a reason we have laws governing the ease with which one can break up a formal marriage. The long-term nature of a marriage brings a lot of efficiency in coordination over time, but it does so only if the marriage lasts long enough for both partners to enjoy the benefits of their joint plans.

If your partnership is likely to be short term, your strategy for coordinating is simpler. If, however, you think someone is going to be your life partner, the amount of coordination you two will want is much greater. The payoff will also be greater, provided you stay together.

This is another example where your *time preference* matters. If you are a "now" sort of person, not concerned much about several years down the road and not interested in planning too much about your future, then it's likely that a long-term partnership with a lifetime companion isn't going to be what you want. That's OK, but you should realize that's the choice you're making.

This orientation toward now or later, your time preference, is something that will be useful if you and your partner agree. If one of you is a now person and the other tends to put a bigger premium on holding off and preparing for later, the two of you will have a lot more difficulty making comfortable decisions together. That's just one of the many things it's good to sort out with a potential partner so you both know where you stand. And, of course, you'll need to know what your own judgment is on this issue before you can be clear about it with anyone else.

Another thing that's different about selecting a partner from the two other big choices we've discussed is that it isn't a choice that has any appropriate timing to it. When it comes to formal education, there's a good reason to get much of it at an early stage in your life. The payoff can then be enjoyed over all the rest of your life, both in your job and in your home. Similarly, for your career, it's beneficial to have a plan fairly early on in life, at least in terms of some areas of interest that you can systematically develop.

But there's less economic or social incentive to select a life partner at a young age. In fact, there are offsetting or competing issues here. On the one hand, it would be sensible to find your partner, to begin to make a life together, and to enjoy the benefits of that close relationship. But on the other hand, as a young person you may not know yet what your own interests will be or just what it is that you can bring to that partnership. So, unlike a job, where you can gain experience and know-how on one job then move on to a better one with your increased skills, getting a life partner is a long-term commitment, so it's best to hold off a while until you know yourself and your options better. That's especially so if the related decision about having children is also one you think you'll put off for a few years.

Your expectations and understandings with your partner about the duration of your relationship are important. They guide how you behave together: what coordination and sharing you engage in, what efforts you both make to split up those substitutable jobs and to engage jointly in those complementary activities.

Because there is relatively little reason to decide about a life partner at a young age, it might be of useful to see at what ages men and women in the United States today make the decision to move in together, as "cohabiting" couples, and at what age most form long-term formal marriages. The tables 4.2 and 4.3 give us an indication of that.

In panel A in table 4.2, we see the remarkable growth over the past few decades in the prevalence of people living together before getting married. Only 11% of women in the age range of 19–44 "cohab-

Table 4.2: Cohabitation by Women Ages 19–44*

Panel A: Percentage of Women Ages 19–44 Who Cohabitated Prior to First Marriage, by Year

Year	Percentage	Year	Percentage
1965–74	11%	1990–94	56%
1975–79	32	1995–99	59
1980–84	41	2000–4	68
1985–89	46	2005–9	66

Panel B: Percentage of Women Ages 19–44 Who Ever Cohabited, by Age and Year

Year	Age				
	19–24	25–29	30–34	35–39	40–44
1987	29%	41%	40%	30%	22%
1995	36	49	50	49	42
2002	38	58	61	59	54
2009–10	38	66	73	66	65

*The figures are reported in Wendy D. Manning, "Trends in Cohabitation: Over Twenty Years of Change, 1987–2010," (FP-13-12), National Center for Family and Marriage Research, Bowling Green State University, 2013. Retrieved from http://ncfmr.bgsu.edu/pdf/family_profiles /file130944.pdf. These are based on three articles: (1) L. Bumpass and J. Sweet, "National Estimates of Cohabitation," *Demography* 26, no. 4 (1989): 615–25; (2) L. Bumpass and H. Lu, "Trends in Cohabitation and Implications for Children's Family Contexts in the U.S.," *Population Studies* 54 (2000): 29–41; and (3) S. Kennedy and L. Bumpass, "Cohabitation and Children's Living Arrangements," *Demographic Research* 19 (2008): 1663–92.

ited" prior to their first marriage in the 1960s and early 1970s, but by the early 1990s, cohabitation was the dominant form of first partnership, with marriage coming later. By now it is pretty common to live together for some length of time before marrying. Panel B of table 4.2 tells us that currently most women have cohabited at some point in their lives before they turned 30. Roughly similar patterns are found for men.

While cohabitation is now a common form of partnership, formal marriage is still very popular. Table 4.3 shows us the popularity of marriage as people age. A pretty small percentage of late teenagers have married, but the rate of marriage rises rapidly during the twenties, with about half of women married by the age interval of 25–29. Men tend to enter their first marriage somewhat later. You'll see that by their late thirties, however, more than two out of three men and women have married.

In fact, throughout the last century and continuing right up to the

Table 4.3: Marital Status, by Age and Gender, United States, 2010

Age	Never Married	Currently Married	Widowed or Divorced
Females			
18–19	95.3%	4.0%	0.6%
20–24	79.3	19.2	1.5
25–29	47.8	47.6	4.7
30–34	27.1	63.8	9.1
35–39	17.7	69.4	12.9
Males			
18–19	97.4%	2.2%	0.4%
20–24	88.7	10.8	0.5
25–29	62.2	34.7	3.1
30–34	36.5	57.1	6.4
35–39	23.5	67.3	9.2

Source: U.S. Census Bureau, Statistical Abstract of the United States: 2012, Table 57: "Marital Status of the Population by Sex and Age: 2010."

present, there hasn't been any generation in the United States that reached their mid-fifties without at least 90% having ever married. For the year 2010, the Census Bureau reports that by the ages 55–65, 93% of women and 91% of men had married.[1]

We see in tables 4.2 and 4.3 that this decision about partnering typically comes along in stages. There is commonly a lot of exploring what it is like to have a close friend, a girlfriend/boyfriend, then a live-in partner, and, only later, a spouse. Some of this exploring is often some of the best times of a young person's life, hanging out, running around with one or several friends, dating, having those deep philosophical conversations or the hotly animated political debates with friends, and occasionally pairing off for more intimate interactions, explorations, and pleasures.

You are as much exploring your own preferences in these activities as you are getting to know the other person. That's the way you find out what's important to you, what your own values are, what you want in your life experiences. Moreover, you can't expect to make a very wise long-term decision until you understand yourself well enough to make clear to your potential partner just what you offer and what you want.

THE MARKETPLACE

We've discussed why you might want to have a partner and what sort of person might be a good one for you. Next let's consider how to get one or how to become one.

Some of the same notions arise here as when you are looking for a job. We can think of there being a marketplace, a location, or a mechanism in which you and others can bring your bundle of personal attributes, talents, interests, and capabilities—what you offer a prospective partner—and the bundle of attributes you hope to find in a partner. In this marketplace, like in others, you search, you negotiate, and if successful, you seal the deal.

Now, in searching for a job, that marketplace is a moderately well-defined thing. It may be an employment office, a computer listing of available jobs, a "job fair" organized to bring the two sides of the market together. And you go to that market with a pretty clear notion that you are, in fact, looking for a job.

The marketplace for a partner can be quite different. It may seem weird to even think of it as a marketplace, but a lot of the same purpose of a job market is at work in finding a partner. Here, the purpose may be less explicit, even hidden—perhaps a dinner party that brings together a likely pair of friends. In other cases such as dating websites, the search motive is very explicit. In this market as in most others, there's competition. Others, too, are looking for a partner, and, like you, they offer some pretty attractive things. But also like you, they have flaws and aren't perfect either. You and they are both looking for a match and displaying what you have to offer. Searching in this market is challenging but can be a lot of fun.

We earlier discussed that there's good reason to look for a mate who complements your interests, capabilities, values, and more. The marketplace for finding a partner is subtly organized to reflect that. There's a song from the musical *South Pacific* that goes, "Some enchanted evening, you may see a stranger, you may see a stranger across a crowded room, and somehow you know, you know even then" that she or he is "the one" for you—love at first sight. That "crowded room," however, is a product of a very sophisticated social organization.

The crowded room might be a party that you and that special stranger both chose to attend. If so, it's likely the party was organized by a mutual friend or around a shared interest, so you two probably have a good bit in common. The organization of social events at school, one's place of worship, some club, or your job brings similar people to the room where they then meet. In that way, the marketplace is remarkably efficient. Markets make searching for most anything, from a car to a job or a mate, much easier.

Schools especially bring together a lot of people who are alike in many ways. In the early stages of this partner-searching business, you tend to run around with friends from school. And typically it is when you are considering the end of your formal schooling, whether it's high school or college or whatever, that you are inclined to select a partner to pair off with. Others who are leaving school at about the same time (and therefore have about the same level of education as you, are about your age, and live in the same neighborhood or chose the same college as you) are likely those to whom you're attracted as a partner. They share much in common with you.

The marketplace for a partner is organized that way, and not by accident. Later, if you go online looking for a partner through a more commercialized environment, you find that there the design is more explicitly purposive, with one website catering to young professionals, another to younger more athletically or more politically inclined men and women, or with one focus or another.

There's a lot to consider as you make your case, as you explore your options. Unlike looking for a job, you may not be sure yet that you even want a long-term partner. The nice thing is that you can approach this choice in stages and look for a partner for the day, for a few hours, for an evening sharing a meal or going to a concert. If that goes well, then you can do it again, or not. You can try with someone else next time or go again with the same person and learn a bit more. Like searching for a job, it's good to have a sensible understanding of what you like and don't like and what you can provide in the way of friendship, humor, knowledge, financial security, or whatever. It might be good to take advantage of the dating marketplace while you are young, but there's another issue that makes it much harder to decide on a life partner while you're still young: uncertainty.

UNCERTAINTY

There are at least three things that are uncertain when you consider choosing a partner. Let's first go through some of the important sources of this uncertainty, then we'll come up with some ways to address it.

First, there's probably a lot, actually, that you don't know about yourself. How will you like being linked to one person as a partner: Will you feel constrained or freed? Will you want to put most of your energy into a job when it gets rolling, or into your relationship with your partner, or maybe into some other project? After getting settled with someone, will you desire a lot of intimacy and closeness, or will you prefer to have a supportive but separate and parallel daily life? Will possessions matter a lot to you? Will an active social life be essential to your happiness?

Second, there's a lot that you don't know about that other person. There are inevitably things that just don't come up when you talk with him or her. He may have keen interests or severe inadequacies that don't get revealed but may make a big difference later on. You can't really know all his aspirations and intentions, or what he'll be like under stress, or when you are ill.

One piece of evidence about the risks involved in this uncertainty is that couples who marry at a very young age—say, under age 18— have a much higher risk of divorce. Specifically, ten years after a marriage, 47% of U.S. women who had married before they turned age 18 had divorced. Of those who married in their early twenties, however, a much lower percentage—27%—had divorced.[2]

The reason seems to be what we were just talking about: young people just don't know enough about their own preferences or capabilities or about what they would like to have in a long-term partner. So they usually don't—they can't—make a very wise choice. As a consequence, their partnerships are a lot less likely to last.

The third thing that's uncertain is what's going to happen as time passes. Will your and his health hold up? Will one of you have an especially hard time with your career, facing layoff and periods of unemployment or really stressful and unrewarding work? Will one of you have spectacular success in your job, rising faster and higher than you now expect? There's also a lot that can happen well beyond the two of you, from natural disasters to economic meltdown to discovering hidden treasure in your backyard.

Research has shown that these unexpected events, whether favorable or unfavorable, tend to destabilize marriages.[3] Whatever happens that wasn't expected tends to increase the chances of divorce. That's true for both positive and negative surprises. The negative ones seem easier to understand. A bad outcome in a job that leads to long-term unemployment, for example, is often linked to divorce. It is true that unfortunate events can bond some couples more tightly together, but, statistically, they more often undermine a marriage.

What's a bit harder to understand is that unexpected good news can have the same destabilizing effect: a career that goes through the roof or a medication that fixes a long-accommodated medical condition tends also to lead to divorce. Perhaps the lucky partner seems to judge the better circumstance as offering new opportunities that would be best undertaken with a different partner. That's one reason movie stars and sports heroes have high divorce rates—the partner who seemed best back when he was barely making it just isn't up to the fast-paced life he now can enjoy: he can do better in the competitive marketplace for a partner now.

There will always be unexpected events, things you and your partner just can't anticipate and plan for. The better the match you've made, the more resilient you two will be when one of those unexpected events occurs. You'll have a bigger buffer, and this implies that the shock, when it comes, will be less likely to wipe out all the benefits from your partnership.

So there's much you don't know, and can't know, when you are considering committing to a long-term partner: you don't know enough about yourself, your partner, or what will happen. In an earlier chapter, we talked about three things you can do in the face of uncertainty. Let's consider them here.

First, try to find out more. In this case, the evidence that those who marry at really young ages are much more likely to divorce suggests one good strategy for reducing the uncertainties: Wait a while before firming up that partnership. Come to know yourself better. Try out some things. Figure out what matters more or less to you and how you handle intimacy, stress, uncertainty, misfortune, and so on. Then, too, the longer you run around with your potential partner, the more you'll find out about him or her. While love at first sight may be a romantic notion (and the way the marketplace is organized may encourage you to think it's happening to you), it's probably best to hold off a bit and not make too strong a commitment until you and your partner have had some time to share a wider set of experiences, to meet more of each other's family and friends.

The second strategy for dealing with uncertainty is to do things that actually reduce risk. Here it's useful to list the uncertainties that concern you and address them one by one. Take the uncertainty of having a decent income stream for you and your family. You might reduce that risk a bit by taking a cue from the advice often given about reducing your financial risks: *diversify*.

You might partner with someone whose career is not in the same industry as your own or who doesn't work for the same company as you do. That will diversify your access to earnings and lower that one risk. Some risks can in fact be directly reduced by your actions. For example, the risk of many health impairments can be lowered by prudent behaviors like not smoking, not drinking to excess, engaging in routine exercise, having a reasonable diet, wearing your seat belt, and not putting yourself or your partner in harm's way. We'll talk more about health habits in chapter 6, but reducing risks to your health lowers the chances of an unexpected event and this in turn will lower the risks to a partnership. If you specify the nature of other uncertainties that you face, they might also be addressed by strategies that reduce the chance of them happening.

The third strategy is to protect yourself against risk. Here, there's a really interesting dilemma. If you "hedge" against some bad event, you don't care quite so much if the bad thing does happen, so you aren't as careful and it happens somewhat more often. So by protecting yourself against an event, you might actually make the event more likely to happen.

That certainly isn't the outcome you want when you protect yourself against risk. One example for which there's good evidence has to do with mandating seat belts in cars, which reduced the likelihood of severe injury or death from a traffic accident. But evidence suggests that when people began wearing seat belts, they drove a little less cautiously and had somewhat more accidents.

Think how this principle works in terms of your uncertainties with your partner. If you consider the risk of a divorce, you might "hedge" a bit by maintaining some of your near-intimate, close friendships with other potential partners. Then, if your relationship with that chosen one doesn't work out, you're covered somewhat. Similarly, it might be best for your relationship to stop taking those week-long fishing trips with the guys and instead spend that time with your partner. But if you think about hedging a little, you may decide to go on that fishing trip, just in case the relationship does fall apart, so you'll still have those fishing buddies.

Every one of these "hedges" that protect you a bit if a partnership doesn't work out also nudges the partnership toward that outcome. Working at a relationship full steam, not hedging, may be best for the prospects of the relationship, but that will mean an even bigger blow to you if it does fall apart. The choice is, of course, yours. And, here again, you really can't have it both ways.

Finally, we've talked about some uncertainties related to having a partner, but there's also a lot of uncertainty if you don't. Living alone puts all the burden on you to earn what you'll need. That imposes some risk. If you hit a patch of bad luck or ill health or something unforeseen, you don't have the protection of a partner who can help keep things together.

SEX PARTNERS

As you read the previous sections about those activities in which you and your partner complement one another, you might well have thought of sex as one of those, so let's talk about that. Hopefully, it is the case that when you have one, your partner and you are indeed "complementary" in the sense we've talked about—making you better at sex in terms of your own enjoyment and your capability in pleasing him or her.

Perhaps you've heard it said that when it comes to choosing a lover, likes attract—there's a lot of evidence that's so. A study of adult Americans found that a very large portion of partnerships are similar in a lot of ways. For example, among married couples in the United States, some 93% are of the same race or ethnicity, some 82% have the same level of education within a couple years, and some 72% share the same religion. What's interesting is that those same high rates apply to couples who are cohabiting.

Perhaps most interesting of all, couples who have been together less than a month and have had sex fewer than ten times also share characteristics: some 91% of those couples are of the same race or ethnicity, 87% are of the same level of education, and 60% share a common religion. Of course, it's also true for all those types of couples when it comes to age—people pair off with someone quite similar to themselves in age, as well as in education, religion, and cultural background.[4] The term for this tendency for similar people to pair with each other is "homophily."

Why do you suppose that is? The primary explanation is what we talked about above: complementarity—there's a lot of communication that goes on during sex and of course a lot of sharing. It is much easier to give and to understand the directives and cues during sex if you and your partner share a common understanding—the most obvious example would be speaking the same language. There are a lot of other aspects of a successful sexual partnership, like sharing an interest in engaging in certain sexual practices or a preference for how often or when to engage in sex, or in deciding whether or not to be exclusive in your sexual relations with that partner. In so many areas, if partners have similar interests and capabilities, the partnership is stronger, it gives greater satisfaction, and typically it lasts longer. That's true about the vacations you take together, the children you raise together, the sexual activity you share, and a whole lot more.

Now, it's important to not interpret this point about homophily too narrowly. Many couples involve two quite different people—in racial or ethnic background, religion, age, size, you name it—and they can be wonderfully successful as a couple, living many years together in great happiness. The facts cited above and the tendency for likes to attract one another is, statistically, the dominant pattern. Evidence suggests that marriages of similar people tend to be more stable. But that is just a tendency, not a certainty. You should not think you are sure to fail if you partner with someone quite unlike yourself, and you can't be guaranteed of success if you partner with someone just like you. The odds of a stable relationship in the long term are a lot better in the latter case, but that's all.

Like in other activities you share with your partner, you learn how to be an effective partner with your lover—you acquire skills and habits that make you a better lover with that partner. Some of those skills may also make you a better sex partner with others, but a lot of the specific stuff you get good at with your partner won't be as effective with another. Different partners will have their own preferences and physical capabilities. Probably the circumstances with another partner will differ also, in terms of your attitude toward pregnancy, your risks of disease, and many other things.

Speaking of the risks of disease, a compelling piece of information that you should consider when making a decision about having sex partners is that those risks rise dramatically with the number of people with whom you have sex. Table 4.4 shows that fact. Panel A shows the relationship between the number of sex partners and the incidence of bacterial and viral sexually transmitted diseases, or STDs. (Bacterial infections include gonorrhea, syphilis, chlamydia, pelvic inflammatory disease, and nongonococcal urethritis; viruses include herpes, human papilloma virus, hepatitis, and HIV/AIDS.)

Let's consider the column labeled "total" in Panel A, which combines the two types of diseases, bacterial and viral, and looks at partners in one's lifetime. We see there that as the number of lifetime sex partners rises from none to 1 to 2–4 partners, the percentage of adults who have had an STD rises from 1.1% to 4.3% to 10.4%. Then as the number of sex partners increases to 11–20, the percentage who have had an STD rises to 33.8%. Finally, for those with more than 20 partners, more than 40% have had one of those diseases.

In panel B we can see the same relationship, but this time looking only at the last 12 months of sexual behavior and of the incidence of disease in that same 12 months. We see exactly the same pattern there: as the number of sex partners over the past 12 months rises from none to 1 to 2–4, and on up to 5 or more, the incidence of having had an STD rises from essentially zero to nearly 6% within the year.

Beyond the obvious connection, it is instructive to consider why

Table 4.4: Sexually Transmitted Infection by Number of Sex Partners (adult ages 18–59)

	Infections		
	Bacterial	Viral	Total
Panel A: Lifetime Infections by Number of Partners Since Age 18			
None	0.0	1.1	1.1
1	2.8	1.7	4.3
2–4	5.8	5.0	10.4
5–10	15.0	9.8	23.4
11–20	24.1	15.9	33.8
21+	30.0	17.7	40.4
Panel B: Past Year Infections by Number of Partners			
None	0.0	0.3	0.3
1	0.6	0.4	1.0
2–4	2.8	1.9	4.5
5+	3.9	2.0	5.9

Source: E. O. Laumann, J. G. Gagnon, R. T. Michael, and S. Michaels, *The Social Organization of Sexuality* (Chicago: University of Chicago Press, 1994), 385–86.

that is so. It turns out that if you list a set of attributes of a sex partner in terms of "familiarity" and "exclusivity," it is the case that the more sex partners an individual has, the less familiarity he or she has with some of them, and the less exclusivity some of those sex partners exhibit. So, for example, if a person has sex with five people, it is very likely that at least one of those five also has five or more partners. The number of people in the network of sex partners doesn't increase from 1, 2, 3, 4, and so on, when you have more partners; it increases more like 1, 4, 9, 16, and so on—almost like the square of the number of partners you have. (That's a little overstated, but you see the point.)

The bottom line is very clear: having more sex partners means more risky partners. It also means that as you have more partners, you have known some of them for a shorter interval of time, so you don't know some of them so well. You are also likely not to know some of them for very long after having sex with them. That, in turn, implies that you and they have a lot less motivation to be protective of one another, so again, the more sex partners you have, the greater risk of disease, and that's just what the table documents.

As you have more partners, at least some of them are themselves riskier in terms of carrying disease and some of them don't have as strong a motivation to be protective of you (or you of them).[5] In terms of the number of your sex partners, it's your choice, of course. But this is one of those instances that involve risk, and in which it is surely true that you bear the consequences of your own choices.

Another risk you want to have in mind when you have sex, of course, is pregnancy. Now, there are times in your life when you will probably want to have a child, and there are probably many other times you'll want to have sex that doesn't result in a pregnancy. The likelihood of a conception from one act of unprotected vaginal intercourse that takes place at a random time in a woman's menstrual cycle is about 3% for a fertile couple. Of course, there are lots of factors that can affect the likelihood of pregnancy. There are things you can do to lower it, and a few that can raise it a bit. Pregnancy is serious business, and we'll focus on some of the decisions related to it in the next chapter, but it is directly related to the choices you make regarding sexual activity.

A couple other choices you'll face in terms of sex are which sex practices you engage in and with what frequency you and your partner have sex. Like so many other elements of your partnership, you and your partner will need to sort these choices out and make decisions that you find satisfying and respectful of each other. This isn't a topic in which accurate data is as easily accessed, so the following couple of tables show you a bit of information that might be of value to you.

When it comes to sex, there are lots of differences in opinions and preferences, so knowing something about how others behave can be helpful to you in many ways. Table 4.5 looks at the incidence of four sexual practices that occurred within 90 days prior to a national survey, by the age and sex of the person.[6]

Table 4.5 shows us that there are differences by age and by gender in some of these practices—men report somewhat higher proportions who masturbate, for example. Both genders suggest that oral sex on men is more common than on women. You'll see that there's nothing in the table that implies that if you do one or another of these things you are unusual. But then you can also read this table as

Table 4.5: Incidence of Several Sexual Practices, by Age and Gender (occurrence within 90 days of the survey in 2009)

Age	Masturbate	Oral (give)	Oral (get)	Vaginal Intercourse
Females				
18–24	50%	58%	55%	68%
25–29	61	64	57	80
30–39	50	52	48	69
Males				
18–24	66%	37%	44%	54%
25–29	77	60	64	80
30–39	71	57	64	79

Sources: For females: Debby Herbenick, Michael Reece, Vanessa Schick, Stephanie A. Sanders, Brian Dodge, and J. Dennis Fortenberry, "Sexual Behaviors, Relationships, and Perceived Health Status among Adult Women in the U.S.," *Journal of Sexual Medicine* 7, suppl. 5 (2010): 277–90, tables 2–4; for males: Michael Reece, Debby Herbenick, Vanessa Schick, Stephanie A. Sanders, Brian Dodge, and J. Dennis Fortenberry, "Sexual Behaviors, Relationships, and Perceived Health among Adult Men in the U.S.," *Journal of Sexual Medicine* 7, suppl. 5 (2010): 291–304, tables 2–4.

indicating that if you don't do one or all of these things, again you are not unusual or exceptional. It's your choice. Don't let anyone convince you that you are odd or exceptional if you do or don't engage in any of these sexual practices.

Based on the same information, table 4.6 shows the frequency of intercourse, again by age and sex and this time by marital status. The principal difference in this table is that the married men and women have sex with much greater frequency than do those who are single. That's not surprising, perhaps, but this emphasizes one of the many attractions to choosing to have a partner. You may also notice that the frequency declines with age for both sexes.

We should also consider another aspect of the choices you make about your sexual relationship with your partner: exclusivity. Some sexual partnerships are based on the understanding of monogamy, of having sex with that one person, your partner, only. Other sexual partnerships don't include that understanding, either because the relationship is more casual or tentative or because the two people both agree that exclusivity isn't important.

Setting aside, at least for the moment, issues of honesty and of religious beliefs, you and your partner face the choice about being exclusive. It's that old issue of scarcity cropping up again: you face a choice and truly cannot have it both ways—you can't be monoga-

Table 4.6: Frequency of Vaginal Intercourse, by Age and Gender and Partner Status

	Single			Married		
Age	None	Up to Weekly	2+ Times a Week	None	Up to Weekly	2+ Times a Week
Females						
18–24	51%	36%	13%	12%	29%	59%
25–29	43	46	11	4	59	37
30–39	72	23	4	6	66	27
Males						
18–24	57%	33%	10%	4%	29%	67%
25–29	47	49	4	2	56	43
30–39	40	47	7	4	63	33

Sources: Same as table 4.5. The detailed frequency is found in table 6 in both papers. Respondents were asked the frequency of vaginal intercourse on average during the past year. The response categories are collapsed here as "None": "not at all"; "Up to Weekly": "a few times per year, once a month, a few times per month, or once a week"; and "2+ Times a Week": "two or three times per week, almost every day, more than once per day."

mous and exclusive with this partner and also have other sex partners. By definition, you can't have both, and actually each has some real attraction.

Being exclusive may mean a lot in terms of your expression of devotion and love and your willingness to sacrifice for your partner/lover. Focusing all your sexual desire and your affection on your partner can strengthen the bond of love between you two. Then too, some of those skills you'll develop as a lover with this partner will develop more quickly and completely if you don't also have any other sex partners where you're developing other types of sexual skills. It is also true that the risk of sexually transmitted diseases is dramatically lower if you have just one partner. (Yes, some of those diseases can be contracted in other ways, like blood transfusions, so this isn't an iron-clad rule, but still . . .) So exclusivity has some real attractions and offers some big-time payoff in terms of your relationship with that partner and in terms of your sense of your own well-being and character.

But then, not being exclusive sexually has some attractions too. They may include the excitement of having new and varied sexual experiences, the constant prospect of meeting someone with whom you'll want to have sexual experiences, maybe the challenge and competitiveness of winning the approval of yet another lover, maybe a higher frequency of having sex. Maybe, too, you'll do some different things sexually with some other partner. So, yes, there are some attractive reasons not to be monogamous. But since you cannot have it both ways, like all the choices we discuss throughout the book, there's scarcity.

Then there's the issue of honesty and fidelity. If you and your partner don't expect or request or promise exclusivity, then you've together made a decision to forgo some of the benefits of monogamy in exchange for some of the benefits of non-exclusive sex. That's a legitimate choice the two of you can make, despite the fact that there are many people in your community who would frown on that choice if they knew of it, and who would argue that it isn't a good thing to do. But throughout our discussion, in every decision we discuss, you are the arbiter of your values, no one else is—not your neighbors, friends, or family, and not even your partner and surely not the author of this book. If you and your partner make a joint decision about this issue of exclusivity, that's that.

What is the case, however, is that if you and your partner decide to promise exclusivity, and each of you expects that of the two of you, then many surveys confirm that most everyone in the country agrees that it is not acceptable to lie, to promise exclusivity and then to violate that promise.

We have talked about sex, but we haven't said much about love. For many people, one, or maybe *the*, main reason for having a sex partner is love. While we've not used the term often or made the point earlier, love has a lot to do with what we've discussed. The affinity toward one another, the complementarity that develops in a longer-term partnership as you and your partner make the effort to become good at what each of you enjoys, the fairness of trading among tasks that either of you can undertake, the longer-term planning of careers, finances, your home, and your kids, and the sharing of your sex lives and your passion all amount to a pretty good, if unromantic, characterization of what love is all about.

Let's focus for a moment on one element of love and sex that bonds the two: intimacy. Intimacy is an attribute of a couple's relationship involving the willful mutual sharing of information that reveals what each person considers his or her deepest nature. Familiarity and trust accompany intimacy and give it value. Intimacy is not always part of a sexual relationship, and intimacy can be experienced by a couple in ways that do not involve sex. Yet a sexual event often involves exposures that have the potential to produce embarrassment and both physical and emotional harm as well as pleasure. The willingness to put oneself in a position to experience these risks, to create these vulnerabilities, and to trust the partner to make positive use of them and not to abuse them are ways in which sex promotes intimacy. To successfully develop and use that trust to produce sexual pleasure creates a sense of self-worth and emotional satisfaction, and it creates affection for the partner who shares that trust. That's a pretty good way to characterize love.

Before we leave the discussion of a sex partner, an additional thought: It will surely be important that you and your partner are sexually compatible and share values, interests, and an eagerness to give and to receive affection. Sex often plays a big role in a couple's growing closer as time passes. But sex is only one and not necessarily the principal element in a fine partnership. Remember our discussion of searching for a job, where you bring a bundle of attributes and capabilities and interests to the labor market and so, too, does the employer, as she has several varied needs to be met by hiring you or someone. It's a challenge to find the right match, one that meshes the bundle of things you bring and are interested in getting with the bundle of requirements and attributes of the job. Well, the same is true when it comes to finding a compatible partner. You have things you're looking for and things you can offer a prospective partner, and so does he or she. Sex is high on your list, perhaps, but it's probably best if you don't let it wholly dominate your choice.

In the bigger scheme of things, sex is only one important element of your choice. If you were choosing a sex partner for one night, then the list of things you might consider would be pretty small and some of those fantasies that pass for preferences in your sex life should probably get real big weight. But if you are considering a long-term partner, the sexual aspects are but one thing to consider, and you'll not want to make your choice, now or in the long run, solely on the basis of sex.

In general, the choice of selecting a partner is necessarily fraught with uncertainty no matter how long or hard you search or how good the match seems to be. But like some other risks, this one may be one worth taking.

THE 1980S COHORT'S MARITAL CHOICES

Taking into consideration all the challenges and uncertainty we've discussed, let's see what the cohort born in the early 1980s are doing in terms of their choices about taking or becoming a partner. Table 4.7 gives us some basic facts.

Overall, we see that by 2009, when they were ages 25–29, 41% of this cohort had married. So it is possible that they will be the first birth cohort in over a century not to have a vast majority who ultimately marry, but we just won't know for another couple decades, especially since the age at which people marry has been rising over time lately.[7]

We see that a much smaller percentage of blacks have married, as is typically found to be the case. Since men tend to marry at an age a few years older than women do, it isn't surprising to see that by the age we are looking at here, fewer men than women have married so far. Panel A also tells us that only a small percentage married before age 17. For blacks and males overall, the percentage who have married before age 20 is less than one in ten.

As if to remind us that not all marriages work out, we see in panel B that more than one in six of those who have married have subsequently divorced. Panel C tells us that of those who have divorced, more than one-quarter of them have already remarried, even more so for whites and for women.

The discussion above points out that marrying at a young age is typically associated with a higher-than-usual rate of divorce, and table 4.8 shows that this tendency holds true for the 1980s Cohort. The table says that the rate of divorce is two or three times as high for those who married younger than age 18 compared to marrying after age 18. You could note that those who married early have had more years at risk of becoming divorced by the time we see them in 2009, so this comparison overstates the difference, but that's not the main reason for the pattern in this table. Marrying at a young age means

Table 4.7: Marriage and Divorce by 2009 (ages 25–29)

	Population	Whites	Blacks	Hispanics	Females	Males
Panel A: Percentage Ever Married and Age at First Marriage						
Ever Married	41.3%	45.5%	22.3%	43.1%	46.6%	36.2%
Age at First Marriage (of those who had ever married)						
< 17	0.4%	0.3%	0%	1.3%	0.7%	0.1%
17–19	11.3	10.8	7.6	16.3	14.9	6.8
20–24	57.7	57.7	56.4	57.8	57.5	57.9
25–29	30.6	31.2	36.0	24.6	26.9	35.2
Panel B: Percentage Ever Divorced and Age at First Divorce						
Ever Divorced (of those who had ever married)	18.6%	18.9%	16.9%	18.2%	19.6%	17.3%
Age at First Divorce (of those who had ever divorced)						
< 20	1.3%	1.1%	0.9%	2.2%	1.7%	0.7%
20–24	48.3	49.0	49.5	42.7	55.8	37.7
25–29	50.2	49.6	49.6	55.2	42.5	61.7
Panel C: Percentage Ever Remarried (of those who had ever divorced)						
Ever Remarried	29.3%	32.1%	14.7%	21.9%	34.7%	21.6%

Source: The 1980s Cohort.

Table 4.8: Divorce, by Age at Marriage, 2009 (ages 25–29)

Percentage Divorced if Age of Marriage Was	Population	Whites	Blacks	Hispanics	Females	Males
< age 18	51.2%	57.8%	—*	36.2%	49.9%	64.0%
Age 18 or older	18.1	18.3	16.9	17.6	18.8	17.1

*Too few cases for this calculation.
Source: The 1980s Cohort.

a lot more uncertainty about the match, and that's the main reason these divorce rates are so much higher among the couples who married quite young.

Cohabitation—living with a partner "in a marriage-like relationship"—has become the living arrangement of choice for a lot of couples, as we saw table 4.2. We can look at the pattern of cohabiting specifically among the 1980s Cohort in table 4.9.

While we saw that only about 41% of this 1980s group had formally married by 2009, we see here that about 63% (38.4 + 24.2) had formed one or more cohabiting partnerships by then. A growing per-

Table 4.9: Cohabitation by 2009 (ages 25–29)

	Population	Whites	Blacks	Hispanics	Females	Males
Panel A: Percentage Ever Cohabited and Number of Cohabitations						
No. of Cohabitations						
Never	37.4%	36.0%	42.4%	38.8%	32.4%	42.3%
1	38.4	39.0	35.9	38.7	39.0	37.9
2+	24.2	25.0	21.8	22.5	28.5	19.8
Panel B: Age at First Cohabitation (of those who have cohabited)						
< 17	2.6%	2.4%	2.6%	4.0%	3.7%	1.4%
17–19	28.6	28.8	24.3	32.9	35.5	20.6
20–24	51.8	51.2	56.8	49.1	47.2	57.1
25–29	17.0	17.6	16.3	14.0	13.6	20.9

Source: The 1980s Cohort.

centage of people cohabited prior to their first marriage, so a lot of those in the "One Cohabitation" row in panel A of this table have subsequently married that partner.

In case you're curious, other research has shown that there isn't a big impact on the likelihood of divorce by whether or not a couple cohabits before they formally marry. Age surely matters, and waiting a few years beyond mid-teenage lowers the risks of divorce, but cohabiting or not doesn't seem to have much effect on the stability of a subsequent marriage in the United States.

We can also look at one or two of the sexual behaviors of this population. Panel A in table 4.10 shows at what age they first had sex (if ever, by 2009), while panel B shows the number of sex partners reported by the time they were 20 years old.

More than half had sexual intercourse with a partner of the opposite sex before turning 17, and a somewhat higher percentage of blacks had done so. As for the number of sex partners by age 20, more than half had one and only one partner. Only a very small proportion reported having more than 10 sex partners by that age, for any of these groups.

As in the earlier chapters, it is interesting to see how a person's family background comes into play, in this case how it corresponds to his or her choice about forming a partnership. Table 4.11 shows the relationship of three of the many elements of family background on

Table 4.10: Sexual Behavior

	Population	Whites	Blacks	Hispanics	Females	Males
Panel A: Age at First Time Having Sex (for those who have had sex)						
< 17	56%	52%	72%	60%	55%	58%
17–19	32	34	22	31	33	30
20–24	10	12	5	8	11	10
25–29	2	2	1	1	1	2
Panel B: Number of Sex Partners by Age 20						
None	2%	2%	3%	3%	2%	2%
1	54	57	44	54	62	47
2	18	18	19	15	19	18
3–5	17	16	22	18	14	21
6–10	5	4	7	6	3	7
11–20	2	2	2	2	1	3
21+	1	1	2	1	0	2

Source: The 1980s Cohort.

Table 4.11: Relationship between Family Background and the 1980s Cohort's Age at First Cohabitation (of those who have ever cohabited)

		Age at First Cohabitation			
	Population	< 17	18–19	20–24	25–29
Panel A: Family Structure at about Age 14					
Intact (parents married)	52%	4%	19%	55%	22%
Parents divorced	12	8	24	56	12
Single parent	9	14	24	49	14
All other	27	9	30	48	13
Panel B: Father's Education Level					
< High school graduate	18%	14%	28%	45%	13%
High school graduate	37	7	24	55	14
Some college (13–15 years)	20	5	20	57	19
College grad+	25	3	17	54	26
Panel C: Frequency of Attending Worship Services at about Age 14					
Never, almost never	17%	9%	29%	49%	13%
Less than once a week	47	7	25	52	16
Once a week or more	36	6	19	55	21

Source: The 1980s Cohort.

one of those choices, the age at first cohabiting. For those that have cohabited, the table shows what percentages did so at each of four age intervals.

We see in panel A that those who grew up with a never-married (single) parent were a lot more likely to cohabit at a young age: 14% compared to only 4% of those that grew up in an intact family, or 8% of those whose parents were divorced. When we look at the father's education level, there is quite a striking pattern. Those whose father had less than 12 years of schooling were a lot more likely to cohabit at an early age than those whose father had more education. We could look at this pattern by the religious affiliation of the parents, but the differences are not very great and are a bit stronger when, instead, we sort by the frequency of parents' attending worship services when our cohort member was about age 14. There, in panel C, we see that there's a bit of a tendency for those whose parents did not attend any worship services to begin cohabiting younger—38% did so before turning 20—contrasted with only 25% of those whose parents attended services weekly.

CONCLUSION

We've spent some time in this chapter on one of the practical reasons most adults live with a partner—it saves money. It's efficient to have a mate since there's a lot to gain in terms of costs of living in sharing your housing, your durable goods like your car, and a lot of your activities with someone else. We noted that if the partnership is expected to be long term, there's even more efficiency from coordinating with your partner. In doing tasks in which one of you can substitute for the other, it's smart for each of you to specialize in some tasks and get better at it while avoiding others that your partner takes on.

In a lot of other activities where you complement one another, it's far more fruitful to do just the opposite and work together to get better at them jointly. That may mean talking things through and deciding what your joint strategy will be, for instance, in raising your kids or saving for retirement.

In considering whom to partner with, it is important to figure out if you and your prospective partner share values and have similar capabilities and interests in those activities in which you'll work together. Important, too, is to be sure that you both have the same expectation and commitment to the length of your partnership, since some of those efforts at coordination don't make sense in short-run partnerships but are terrifically valuable if it is a long-term deal. You need to know for yourself what you expect, and then you need to be forthright and clear in sharing that expectation with your partner, as, indeed, he or she needs to be with you in return.

We've discussed the importance of that ever-present issue of now or later. It is helpful if you and your partner have a pretty similar judgment about that issue. If one of you is more inclined to wait while the other of you is more inclined to go for it now and not worry so much about later, that is likely to get in the way of reaching agreement on a lot of the bigger issues you'll face together. Do you like to wait and buy that big item after you've saved up for it? Are you inclined to make some sacrifices now in the expectation that they will pay off well in the years ahead? Are you one who likes to avoid risks today that may seem like fun but can mess up your life later if they go badly? It's good if you and your partner agree on things like this.

Similarly it's helpful if the two of you basically agree on a lot of other preferences, such as how social or private you'll want to be or how much risk you'll be willing to take in your financial planning or careers. The more you can figure out about how this will work for you and your partner before you form a relationship, the more likely it will be that the partnership works out well. That's one reason for delaying forming a partnership until you have some of this figured out for yourself. We've seen that those who get married at a very early age are far more likely to divorce, and the reason seems to be a lack of insight about what they offered their partner or what they wanted in return.

You might be disappointed that we've not focused more on some of the feelings associated with forming a solid partnership—the love, affection, devotion, trust, and respect that accompany a successful partnership, or the passion and desire that are a big part of it. That is what we've been talking about, just with a different language, since the feelings of attraction for your partner, the pride you feel in his or her successes, and the good fortune you feel in having him or her as your partner develop from the efforts you each make to find those complementary activities, to share those aspirations, to commit to those mutual goals, and, yes, to express that love in passionate and caring ways.

You'll need some balance in all this as neither the passion alone nor the "productive efficiencies" alone make for a good partnership. This choice of a partner is challenging, and making a reasonably smart choice is important for you and for your partner—and if it results in some children, for them as well. So don't overlook one aspect or focus on only one element of this decision.

And don't forget to have some fun along the way—in making this choice, there's a lot of room for enjoyment in the searching and exploring. Bring those abstract values you've committed to—integrity, compassion, fairness, or whatever you have as your values—to bear in your decisions about whether or not to have a long-term partner and just who that will be.

| # Parenting

Your children need your presence more than your presents.

JESSE JACKSON

Few of the big decisions you'll make in your life have greater impact than the decision to have a child. The role of parent is a quintessential "adult" role. The choices we discussed in previous chapters all involved decisions to acquire something—an education, a career, or a partner. The choices you face in having and rearing children are different.

In this chapter we'll address a couple distinct aspects of parenting. First is the choice about whether or not to have children and if so at what age and how many. The second is the decision about the nurturing and rearing of your children. Some of the same ideas and concepts are useful in considering both of these decisions, so after reflecting on a few facts about each, we'll focus on those concepts and see where they apply.

If you have any doubt that scarcity is a fact of life, when you have a child that doubt will disappear—raising a small child will reveal scarcity of things you didn't even think about having. Yes, kids cost a lot of money and, yes, they take a lot of time, too, but you'll probably find you have a real scarcity of patience, energy, and knowledge of all those things about which your child asks you, "Why?" Even the time to get a night's sleep is scarce when your child is having growing pains of one sort or another.

Yet, for centuries, despite the costs and the burden, men and women have chosen to have and to raise children, and more often than not they'll tell you that it was the most rewarding and fulfilling role they ever played. So regardless of just how conscious the choice was, for most parents it seems to be one that is viewed favorably in retrospect.

BECOMING A PARENT

You can't inadvertently get an education or a career or even a partner, but it happens sometimes that one discovers that a pregnancy has resulted without making any real effort. There you are, moving along toward one of life's most demanding, costly, and potentially rewarding adventures, and you haven't given it much thought at all. So one of the central questions you'll want to consider is whether or not you want to have children. We'll talk about the costs and the benefits of doing so, but first some facts to have in mind.

A sizable proportion of the adult population actually does not ever become a biological parent: in recent years about one in six females in the United States reach menopause having not had a child.[1] For a large portion of those women, it was an overt, conscious choice. For others, it was less a direct decision than a result of a medical limitation of theirs or their partner or not having a heterosexual partner. That reminds us that one can wish to have children, but for one of several reasons find it exceptionally difficult or impossible.

A recent study estimated that among married couples of childbearing age, some 6% were infertile, and an additional 12% had an impaired ability to conceive.[2] In recent years, couples who previously found it very difficult or impossible to have their own children can now do so with the increased use of assisted reproductive technology, which in 2011 was used for more than 1% of births in the United States.[3] These procedures are used not only by couples with impaired fertility, but also by gay and lesbian couples who wish to have children. The cost of these procedures is substantial, in money, time, and inconvenience. Their use attests to the strong desire many people have to bear and rear their own children.

At the same time, it is also the case that many others who have actually had children did not consciously choose to have them. One of the top research institutions on reproductive health, the Guttmacher Institute, estimates that a little over half of the 6.6 million pregnancies in the United States each year are unintended, and that by age 45, more than half of all American women will have experienced an unintended pregnancy. The concept of "unintended" pregnancy includes those that are either unwanted or "mistimed," and about 60% of those unintended pregnancies were mistimed but not unwanted sometime. Unfortunately, the rate of unintended pregnancies is about six times higher for women in poverty than for those well above poverty.[4]

Even for those who choose to have children, even several of them, the proportion of one's fertile lifetime in which one wants to become (or get someone) pregnant isn't very large. Sexually active heterosexuals have a choice about how vigilantly to do the things that reduce the risk of a pregnancy. Sexual practices can affect that risk. The use of contraception can too. The Guttmacher Institute points out that of the women who experienced those unintended pregnancies, only 5% were consistently using contraception, 43% were using contraception inconsistently, while 52% were not using contraception at all. When used consistently, contraception works well, and since the cost of having a child is so high, it sensible to make an effort to avoid a pregnancy that's unintended.

There's another matter that arises here that involves a choice, often a wrenching choice: whether or not to have an abortion when faced with an unintended pregnancy. This is one of those choices for which no amount of information about what others have chosen to do, or about what the medical facts are, can offer perfect clarity about what choice to make. It is an intensely personal choice for the pregnant woman and often her partner. There's no universally right or wrong decision about this choice.

Circumstances of all sorts may influence the choice—medical, religious, economic, social, psychological, and more. Probably no one wants to get into a position where a choice about an abortion must be made—it is a matter of selecting one or another rather bad option, the one that seems to be the least unattractive. Perhaps the best counsel is to seek advice and talk it through, know what the relevant outcomes are likely to be, and then judge those circumstances and make your own decisions as a couple or as an individual, as is appropriate.

Maybe a few facts can begin to provide some guidance, but they won't tell you what's right for you. The Guttmacher Institute provides some of the best factual information on the incidence or frequency of abortions in the United States. They tell us that of the half of pregnancies in the United States that are unintended, 40% are terminated by abortion. Annually a little under 1% of women ages 15–44 have an abortion, and about half of them have had at least one previous abortion. They also tell us a bit about the women who have abortions, indicating that 37% identify as Protestants and 28% as Catholics. Women who have never married and are not cohabiting account for 45% of all abortions in the United States, and 61% of abortions are obtained by women who have one or more children.[5]

Another relevant finding is that women who become pregnant appear to weigh the economic and social consequences of having a child when deciding whether to have an abortion. Those who are unmarried, are quite young, and have highly educated parents are more likely to have an abortion—for them, the costs of having the child are especially high.[6]

Finally, there is an additional option that arises both for women who are unintentionally pregnant and also for ones who wish to have a child but cannot: adoption. Currently around 135,000 children are adopted in the United States each year, and 2–3% of all U.S. citizens have been adopted. While we more often hear of children adopted from foreign countries, about 59% of American adoptions are from the U.S. child welfare or foster care systems.[7] You will find in the appendix that 1% of the 1980s Cohort that we're following have themselves been adopted (see table A.8).

So, there are indeed many choices here, and while at times it may seem there aren't many good options or a lot of frustration and anxiety surrounding the issues of pregnancy and having a child, there can be pretty attractive options to consider. These are important choices, for you and your partner—and the potential child—so you'll want to give this one a lot of thought.

The choice about having children is only the first of the choices one faces about becoming a parent. The second decision is when. At what stage of life will you choose to take on this responsibility? You could do it as a young, energetic teenager, or when you've finished school, or after establishing a career and firming up your marital partnership. The timing in your life for your childbearing is an important issue, worthy of a lot of consideration. In the United States overall, the average age of a mother at the birth of her *first* child has been rising quite a lot in recent decades—from about age 23 in 1980, 24 in 1990, 25 in 2000, and 26 in 2013.[8] This reflects the fact that teenagers are less likely to have children today and that the number of women in their mid-thirties and older who are having their first child has been rising.

Then there's the choice about how many children you intend to have. One can find arguments why one, or two or three or several is best, and there are many aspects of this choice, including the spacing of the kids. In the United States, the average number of children women have had by the age of 45 has remained steady at about two children over the past quarter century, but was much higher in decades past. For the most recent year available, 2014, for women ages 45–50, about 17 percent of women had no children, 19 percent had one, 34 percent had two, and 31 percent had three or more, which averages out to about two.[9]

Let's spare you so many facts about the care and nurturing of children except to point out that families do differ quite a lot in how much time, money, and attention they devote to their children, so there's much choice here as well. There's a wide span of what that choice might be within the socially acceptable range that excludes deprivation and child neglect, on the one hand, or excessive pampering and unhealthy shielding of the child financially or socially, on the other. Just one statistic about this: one study estimated that a quarter of people in the United States live in families that spend less than $30 per child for every $100 spent on the adults, while another quarter of them live in families that spend more than $45 per child for every $100 spent on the adults.[10] Families differ a lot on their spending on their children compared to their spending on the adults. And the variation in the money spent relative to the money spent on the adults is probably smaller than the variation in the *time* spent with the kids, relatively, across families. So in addition to the choice about whether, when, and how many children to have, there's the all-important choice about how to raise your children, how to be a parent.

Fortunately, there are several useful ideas that can offer guidance about many of the choices we've just mentioned. Let's consider some of them.

THE COST

In chapter 2 we discussed the distinction between the cost and the price of an item. The distinction arises when its producer isn't the same as its consumer. In the marketplace where the item is traded or sold, the distinction makes a lot of sense. When it comes to a child, there is surely a cost to the parents, but it doesn't make much sense to talk about the price since, fortunately, children are typically not sold.

The cost of a child isn't set by some corporation or government or even by the marketplace, but by the decisions families make about their own expenditures of money and time and lots of their other resources on their kids. There are many choices here and many differences in what's spent by one family or another. For many years, the federal government has put out a terrific booklet each year that tells what they calculate an American family spends in money (but not time or other things) on kids. They do so for children of each year of age, since what's purchased for an infant or a toddler isn't the same stuff as that for an elementary school–aged child or a teenager.

As you might suspect, the amount spent by a family at a pretty low level of income is a lot less than families with higher levels of income, as table 5.1, from that government publication, shows. You'll see in that table how the costs vary by the age of the child and by the family's income level. The publication tells us that the costs are higher for the first child than for the second or third. If you are interested in more detail, I recommend you look up that booklet.[11]

That publication also tells us what those expenditures are. The biggest is housing (about 30% of the total expenditure on a child), followed by child care and education (18%), food (16%), transportation (14%), health care (8%), clothing (6%), and then anything else (the remaining 8%). While these amounts reflect the spending by husband-wife families, there are somewhat different amounts spent by one-parent families and differences by the region of the country.

So a child costs a lot. And this is the annual cost, so you'll expect to be spending something between $10,000 and $20,000 each year for the child, up to age 18. (The costs don't end then—far from it— but the government publication only provides information on the expenditures up to that age, and it also notes that it does not include

Table 5.1: Estimated Annual Expenditures on a Child by Husband-Wife Families, by Family Income (before tax), and by Child's Age, 2013

Age of Child	Family Income		
	< $62,000	$62,000–107,000	> $107,000
0–2	$9,480	$12,940	$21,430
3–5	9,520	12,970	21,440
6–8	9,130	12,800	21,330
9–11	9,950	13,680	22,290
12–14	10,370	14,420	23,750
15–17	10,400	14,970	25,700
Total (0–17)	176,550	245,340	407,820

Source: Mark Lino, *Expenditures on Children by Families, 2013* (U.S. Department of Agriculture, Center for Nutrition Policy and Promotion, Miscellaneous Publication No. 1528-2013, 2014), table 1, p. 26, http://www.cnpp.usda.gov/Publications/CRC/crc2013.pdf.

the pre-birth medical care costs.) And the scary fact is, because children also take a lot of time, which also has a cost, the dollar cost is really only about half the total cost.

Estimating the *time cost* of a child is even more difficult than figuring out the money cost. The way it's typically done is to get a sense of the time involved, and then use the person's wage rate as an indication of how to put a value on those hours. We'll not spend a lot of time on this, but one good study concluded that the cost of time spent on raising a child was higher than the dollar expenditure each year.[12] Several other studies have reached essentially the same conclusion, so you'll have to double that $10,000 to $20,000 annual dollar cost if you want to approximate the annual total cost of a child. That time cost is spent in many varied activities, some of which are terrifically fun and others that are definitely boring and tedious, and they differ a lot from one family to the next in both how the time is spent and what the value of those hours might be.

We talked about the *opportunity cost* of going to college, the fact that spending time there has a real cost in terms of what it is you have to forgo to attend college. Well, the same is true in terms of these time costs of having and raising a child. Whether the next best use of your time is working for pay, going dancing, or sleeping, there's a real cost to your time spent with your child.

Let's put a couple of things we discussed earlier together here:

Table 5.2: Fertility by Education Level

Panel A: Average Number of Children Ever Born, Ages 22–44, by Gender and Schooling Level (2006–2010)

	Women	Men
No high school diploma	2.5	1.7
High school diploma or GED	1.8	1.3
Some college	1.5	1.0
Bachelor's degree or higher	1.1	1.0

Panel B: Completed Fertility for U.S. Women Ages 40–50, June 2012

	Children Ever Born
Not a high school graduate	2.6
High school graduate	2.1
Some college, no degree	2.0
Associate's degree	1.9
Bachelor's degree	1.8
Graduate or professional degree	1.7

Panel A Source: Gladys Martinez, Kimberly Daniels, Anjani Chandra, "Fertility of Men and Women Aged 15–44 Years in the U.S.: National Survey of Family Growth: 2006–2010," *National Health Statistics Reports*, no. 51 (April 12, 2012): fig 1, p. 5.
Panel B Source: Lindsay M. Monte and Renee R. Ellis, "Fertility of Women in the United States: 2012," *Current Population Reports* P20-575 (Washington DC: U.S. Census Bureau, July 2014), table 2.

those with more schooling have a high wage rate in the job market, so that means that those with more education have a higher opportunity cost of time spent with their child. This is one reason we see that more educated people typically have fewer children: the children cost more in terms of the parent's time.

Table 5.2 shows this relationship based on a recent national survey in the United States. Note, however, that this is a survey of quite young people, so they have many more fertile years ahead of them. Panel B shows us the fertility for an older age group of women in the United States. There we see the same decline in number of births as education rises. It is a much smaller difference in panel B since the more educated women by age 40 or so have had time to have more births than shown in panel A. I mentioned earlier that the number of children that women have in the United States today has averaged around two kids and that this number is a lot lower than it was in decades past. One of the main reasons for that reduction in the number of children is that as women's schooling levels have gone up, so, too, have their earnings in the labor market, and this means that the cost to them of having children has risen. At the higher costs of children today, many choose to have fewer.

Taking all these costs into consideration, the money cost and the opportunity cost, if you add them up for a child over his first 17 years, you'll see that the total cost is probably more than you'll consider spending on the home that you might buy. Kids cost a lot! But there are several pretty interesting differences between the payment for a house and the payment for a child.

The first thing is that you'll consider the whole cost of a house before you buy it, and you and the seller (or builder) will basically agree on the cost you'll face in acquiring the house. Your baby doesn't sit down and negotiate the cost with you (nor does your ob-gyn doctor or your partner). In fact, as we just admitted, it's really quite difficult even for social scientists or the government to calculate just what a child costs, but the housing cost is explicit, definite, and easily ascertained not only by you but by others who care to look it up.

Also, the house payment is one you'll have to arrange up front, either by paying for it directly (which few people can afford to do) or by paying a percentage of the cost and borrowing the remainder, typically from a bank in the form of a many-year mortgage with an agreed-upon interest rate. Both the house and the child may obligate you to make payments for 20 or so years, and the magnitude of the total cost may not be all that different, but the payment arrangements are very different, as is whom you owe, how you pay, and what happens if you fail to pay. And when you buy a house, you make a very conscious decision to buy—no one inadvertently wakes up some morning and finds she's bought a house!

Another distinction is that you can reverse your decision later and sell your house. That's not really an option with a child. You may consider having a child as an investment, sort of like buying a house, but it is an "illiquid" investment. You can't take it back to the marketplace where you got it (or anywhere else for that matter) and sell it back later, as you can with a house. That's one reason this choice is such an important one. It is essentially irreversible, likely to last the rest of your life. It is costly in so many respects—and breathtakingly rewarding in most cases.

Taking the idea of a child as an investment a bit further, if you do think in those terms, you'll notice that unlike the investment in a house, there's no real chance that you'll ever get your money back. The payback is in other currencies than cash. Most parents would consider their investment in their children well worthwhile, but the rewards come in the joy of having a child, of interacting with her over the rest of your life, of seeing her grow up and find her way in the world, of watching her express her interests and make her contribution to society.

A child may bring you lots of happiness and pride and satisfaction, perhaps, but probably not a monetary reward. It's possible that when you're much older, your child will be in a position to provide some economic security and psychological and emotional support and satisfaction to you, but that's not the same sort of currency in which you might hope to benefit from an appreciated value of your house and property. Your investment in a child may actually provide you a much bigger return, but, in most cases, it won't be financial.

There are real attractions to having your own child in terms of continuing your family history from your generation forward, experiencing the deep satisfaction of guiding your own baby into healthy adulthood, enriching your own and your partner's life by the love, caring, and sharing of experiences with your child, and the joys of discovery as your child grows up. Like so many life choices, you'll need to weigh these benefits and costs and reach a judgment about becoming a parent. The mistake would be to disregard one of the key elements in the decision, either the considerable costs involved or the considerable benefits and attractiveness of being a parent.

Even though a child might cost more than a house, you may well decide it's time for you to take on the responsibilities of becoming a parent—time now to devote a large portion of your time and energy to nurturing and raising a child. Indeed, a majority of adults do undertake that responsibility at some point, and we all are here because someone did so for each of us. Remember that it is a big choice, however, with a lot of repercussions for you and for the child for many years to come, so it deserves to be given careful consideration. You shouldn't be casual or cavalier about starting your role as a parent. It is too important and too demanding for that.

And as if the choices here weren't already challenging enough, there's something that we haven't directly addressed yet—having a baby takes two! This means at least two things: first, you must choose with whom to have this baby, and, second, the decision isn't all or exclusively your own if you have a partner, since your partner has a right—and probably a desire—to play a role with you in making the decision about whether, when, and how many children to have.

In the discussion about choosing a partner, we noted that if it's more than a very temporary matter, the decision involves a lot more than just your sexual compatibility, since you'll be sharing much of your life with this person. Same here: the decision about the right guy or the right gal with whom to have the baby is an important part of the decision about your fertility.

Traditionally, one's life partner and co-parent was the same person, and that's still the case for a vast majority, but no longer so for all. The medical technology of fertilization and the social-sexual decisions about same-gendered partnerships have unlinked those two choices for some adults today. If you are in the traditional mode, you will be selecting one partner, and that person will be your sex partner and the biological co-parent of your child, as well as your financial partner and general companion through life. If your choice of a life partner is not of that traditional heterosexual sort, you'll still have the obligation to coordinate with your life partner about whether and when to have a child, and maybe even the issues of the biological co-parent.

Boy, this gets complicated, doesn't it? Whenever the issue of whether and when to have that first child comes along, it involves your partner's judgments and preferences in addition to your own. It may be that you find broad agreement with your partner. If not, this is one of the areas where you are not so free to act on your own. You'll need to work through differences of opinion and reach some outcome acceptable to the two of you, if you have a partner.

PRESENT-FUTURE

Like the other choices we've considered, there's a strong now-or-later element to the decisions about your fertility. That's true of the risks you might chose to expose yourself to in terms of having sex in the first place, to the decisions you make about what to do if you and your partner learn of an unexpected or unintended pregnancy, and to many of the decisions you make about how you'll handle the responsibilities of parenthood. What is likely to be the easiest or most attractive action in the very short run may not lead to the longer-run outcome you want to have—if they are the same, there's no choice to be made, happily. That's not always the case, however. Often you face the choice of a better thing now or later.

The choice about the timing of when you have children is greatly affected by whether or not you've found the partner with whom you wish to have your family. Then, too, the timing is all wrapped up with the timing of several of the other big decisions you face, including the completion of your formal schooling and getting under way with your career. There's been a lot of discussion and advice offered in the popular press about whether it's better to have your children before you get too immersed in your career or whether it's best to wait, get some useful experience on a job, establish your work credentials, and then take time to start your family. There's no simple answer. It depends on the career plans and family circumstances you and your partner have.

This is an example of that "putty and clay" issue: malleable or flexible opportunities and choices at one stage of your life inevitably lead to some more rigid conditions later when those earlier choices have been acted upon. So if you take on debt to complete your formal schooling, you may find it necessary to earn enough now to pay off some of those loans, and this may suggest waiting a while before becoming a parent. Maybe some other element of your life may indicate that the time to start a family is sooner rather than later. For example, maybe your extended family will be living nearby for only a few years and they'll be able to help you with your kids if you have them soon. The choice is yours.

Another rather interesting issue that's all tied up with the choice about when to have children and when to begin your career is especially relevant for women. At the beginning of the chapter, I mentioned that about one in six women reached menopause without having any children. That percentage for women born in 1955 was twice as high as it was for women born fifteen years earlier, in 1940. Those fifteen years were the ones in which women greatly expanded their formal schooling and their entry into the workforce. A key reason for the rise in childlessness over those years was the fact that the cost of children was rising as women's opportunities in the workforce increased.

As the costs of children rose—the opportunity costs in this case—more women avoided having children.[13] It's also the case that there was a big decline in the number of children born over that time span to women who already had children. Overall, the general fertility rate for the U.S. population fell almost every year for the twenty years beginning in 1957, a period of rapid growth in female education levels and labor force participation. Costs matter, and both time costs and money costs influence choices about births.

Another distinction between the choice about acquiring education and having children is that for education one makes a substantial investment up front and expects to enjoy a return on that investment over the subsequent years. With children both the costs borne and the benefits from having the child are spread out quite differently than with education, a bit more evenly over time for both the costs and the benefits. This choice, then, doesn't depend as strongly on your time preference, since the costs and benefits flow along year by year. Don't forget, though, that this decision is quite long-term—it isn't one you can easily reverse if you change your mind.

When it comes to the decision about how many children to have, one thing that makes it a bit easier is that it can be considered sequentially—you don't have to put in your order for the number you want all at once. You can get started at some point, and after you've had a child and gained some experience, you can make your next decision about whether or not to have more. One thing that's at work here is that the second child and any subsequent children cost somewhat less because of lifestyle, household goods, and especially the time it takes to oversee the kids when they are young. It's those economies of scale again, which were discussed in the previous chapter.

HUMAN CAPITAL

In most of the activities in which you engage throughout your life, you decide how much of your effort and intellect, your muscles and psyche, you'll put into that task. You know that when you worked harder on a school project, with more hours and greater concentration, you learned more and probably got better grades. It's that old adage: "The more effort you put in, the more you'll get out of it." That's true at your job and just as true of your friendships and your garden. It's also true of your children.

However, there's a profound difference between applying that truism to your garden and to your children. You don't inherently care about the well-being of your garden. But you do care how your children do in life, how well prepared they are for the challenges they'll face and the opportunities that come along.

By deciding to become a parent, you take on the responsibility to raise your child—a deep responsibility that goes to the core of your being, in taking care of them, in protecting and nurturing them. After all, the decision you made to have a child wasn't one he or she participated in. You and your partner made that choice, but how it turns out impacts your child as well as you. Unlike the carrots and beans in your garden, almost certainly you care deeply about that child.

So here's a really hopeful bit of information that's backed up by evidence from many researchers. You have the resources and capacity to have a profound influence on your child.

Whatever your own state of well-being economically or psychologically or socially, you can do a lot to help your child, and your influence persists throughout his life. Sure, it's nice if you have a lot of income or social standing in your community. Children do benefit from that. They can attend better schools, live in greater relative comfort, experience a wider set of things, and eat a higher grade of beef. And, yes, those things matter. But so, too, do the things that you can give your child that don't take money. Let's talk about a few examples.

It's well documented that an unborn child can be badly harmed if its mother drinks or smokes while she's pregnant. These exposures impact the healthy development of the fetus and can have a lifelong impact. Convincing evidence tells us that the mom's exposure to alcohol during her pregnancy shows an effect on her child even years later, such as how many years of school the child will complete, the likelihood he'll attend college, even how much he earns over the age of 30—a long time after the in utero exposure to alcohol.[14] (And yet an authoritative source within the NIH tells us that some 20–30% of women in the United States drink at some point during their pregnancy.[15])

Apparently, exposure to alcohol and to the toxic chemicals in tobacco is detrimental to the growth and development of the fetus even at very early stages of development, including before the woman typically knows that she is pregnant. The convincing evidence that tobacco is harmful to the fetus—in terms of fetal and neonatal mortality, birth weight, and cognitive capacity as the child grows up—has been publicized for over 40 years.[16] It doesn't take any money to not smoke and to not drink alcohol. It may take determination, and that's why your motivation as a parent is so important.

We've discussed various reasons why you may in fact decide to have a child. But there's likely to be another motivation, and that is a highly selfless instinct to bring that child into the world and give it your love, the attention it needs and desires, and to nurture and provide for the child and help it grow into a balanced and healthy person. This is the motivation you will want to think of if tempted to smoke or drink alcohol while you are pregnant.

There is also compelling evidence that exposure to certain chemicals, like lead in the air we breathe, can have a big impact on a young child. There's wonderfully strong evidence that when countries took the lead out of gasoline used in automobiles, the health of young children improved pretty dramatically. By now the long-term effects on children are documented, and they show that lower exposure to lead in the air has resulted in notably higher grades in school, higher high school graduation rates, and higher labor-market earnings for children some 20 or more years later.[17] That's one example of an issue that parents themselves didn't need to take on, since the whole community, the whole society, addressed it. But the drinking of alcohol or the exposure to cigarette smoke and several other chemical are choices that the mother and sometimes the father, not the community, decide.

After a child is born, there's a lot of evidence that breast-feeding has some important and long-term positive impact on the child. If it's physically feasible for the mother, it's not something that takes money, even though it does take a lot of patience and planning (not a direct dollar expenditure, but another opportunity cost).[18] Then there are the unglamorous but really important things parents, both parents, can do with the child in terms of spending time reading, talking, playing, encouraging, nudging, and responding to her.

There's evidence in a non-human species that when a caregiving mom tends her offspring, the chemicals in the offspring's brain change. Scientists presume this is due to greater comfort and a lower sense of stress experienced. And there's clear physical evidence that this chemical change, based on an offspring's experience with its caregiver in the first seven days of life, impacts the offspring's behavior for its whole lifetime.[19] Now, humans may not work quite like that, but the point is that nurturing and caring parents can impact children in ways that help them develop coping skills, their personality, and their ability to function effectively in society.

There's lots of evidence that while money or financial prosperity is beneficial in terms of a child's cognitive skills and well-being, so, too, are the simple, doable behaviors and habits by parents. These include being attentive, engaging with the child, connecting with his interests and concerns at the time he expresses them, explaining why this is so or that is not so, and why that person is doing what he's doing, on and on over the months of the child's youth. These simple activities that engage with the child can have a big impact.

Evidence suggests that when a family has a relatively low level of financial or material resources, these acts of parental engagement with the child are particularly effective and influence the child's ability in reading and math years later.[20] That should be a powerful motivator for less-well-off parents. You should understand that you can have a major impact on your child's development and life success.

You can't mold his personality, but you can influence it somewhat. You cannot hand him a high IQ, but there's a lot of evidence that a parent can influence the measured intelligence by several IQ points, and that's enough to make a difference. You can't hand your child all that he will need, and at times this is one of the most frustrating realizations in your life. But you do have influence; you can move the dial. You and your partner have the best chance of anyone to do that for your child. Others—teachers, friends, mentors—will play roles, both good ones and bad ones. But as a parent, you get the lion's share of the opportunity to give your child a good start.

But despite your love for your child and your acknowledgment that you've got an enormous responsibility, you may also have a lot of other important things going on in your life just then. You may decide that you'll wait a while and make that big push on your child's behalf at a later time, when it's a bit more convenient for you and when he's a bit older and can use your efforts all the more.

Here's the thing: The timing of the efforts on behalf of your child matters a lot; *earlier* in his lifetime is better than later. So here we have run into another of those hard choices that you'll confront throughout your life. While your time preference or your personal circumstances may suggest that you wait and make a big push to help your child later in his life, the fact is that earlier is better for your child, so you'll have to decide.

There's a reality out there that is not connected to your preferences. It, like those preferences, needs to be considered when you make your choice. In this case, the reality is that an early effort with your child has the biggest impact on him. That principle even applies to the time before he is born, as we've discussed—those efforts his mom makes to avoid harmful chemicals probably have the biggest payoff in terms of later well-being. It's also true that the first couple years of life matter more than later. The reasons seem to be that in both brain development and habits of behavior, if your child learns something early, he can use that knowledge as he learns other things. The more he has learned previously, the greater the rate at which he learns as the months go by.

This is a little like compound interest: the higher the rate at which he learns things as a tiny infant, the more he will learn a few months later, and the same as he gets still a little older, and on and on. To start him out with considerable cognitive stimulation and a fulsome response to all his curiosity enable him to want to know more, to be able to absorb more, and to continue to expand his awareness and capabilities. As one of the scholars who studies this concluded from his research, "learning begets learning."[21]

One additional thought about this issue of making a big commitment to nurturing your child at an early age. One thing a parent must decide with the birth of the child is whether or not to stay home with the child and not have the time-consuming obligation of a job while the child is very young. There's been a lot of research on whether or not that matters in terms of the child's future well-being. The bottom line seems to be that it does not matter a lot whether a parent stays home with the infant or toddler.

There is clear evidence that children need and greatly benefit from sustained and nurturing stimulation and, above all, they need a reliable and stable environment and a lot of unconditional love and attention. But working moms and dads can give that love and offer that stability while also using other caregivers. The employment-or-not decision isn't the key factor; the love and attention, the stability and predictability of care seem to be key.

Talking about the time and efforts you make with your child as an investment may seem strange, even inappropriate, as if it isn't a loving or caring thing you're doing or that the only reason you'll do it is for the return on the investment. That's not the real issue, of course. Your love and affection and concern and good wishes for your child are what matter most. But thinking of these efforts as having a real payoff for you and your child later in his life gives useful guidance about just when and how important it is to make the big effort for the child. The "rate of return" on the investment has been shown to be greater if the investment is made at an earlier age. The investment of money and time and love do have a profound impact on your child. That's the useful guidance based on a lot of good research.

UNCERTAINTY

When it comes to having children, there are a lot of unknowns, most of which you can't really control. From the gender of your child to his or her personality, intellectual capabilities, looks, size, and on and on, there's much that lies well beyond you and your partner, no matter how carefully you plan and how much effort you expend. The scope of what you don't know is awesome, and it might discourage you from even having a child.

One fact that's not widely known and emphasizes just how much uncertainty there is surrounding this topic is how many conceptions end spontaneously. Medical science tells us that "around half of all fertilized eggs die and are lost spontaneously, usually before the woman knows she is pregnant. Among women who know they are pregnant, the miscarriage rate is about 15–20%. Most miscarriages occur during the first 7 weeks of pregnancy."[22]

Despite all the uncertainty, most people do have children, and while they probably aren't all that much better at parenting than you, their kids seem to turn out OK, most of the time. The world into which children are born is troubling as well, with an awful lot of things that seem to have gone wrong and may seem likely to get even worse. But again, you can't do much about it, and you never know just how bad or good the circumstances will be for your child down the road.

This book's author was born a few weeks after the awful moment in U.S. history when the Japanese nation attacked the U.S. Navy fleet at Pearl Harbor, Hawaii, and the world seemed to be in a pretty bad state about then—not a time you'd like to be born, it might seem. But the decades following have been ones of unparalleled economic success for the United States and actually quite a lucky time to have grown up, with the GI Bill helping many young adults get their education in the 1950s, a "baby boom" following the end of World War II that helped propel our nation, coupled with technological advances that would have been beyond the dreams of couples making their fertility decisions in the pre-WWII era of discouraging economic depression. From a global perspective, you can't really know when the right time is for starting your family. The choice you make probably should be based on more personal circumstances and preferences, not the uncertain state of the world.

We've talked about how to approach uncertainty in other domains—you can learn a lot about it and what its implications are for you, so you can assess how it should impact your choices. You can often do some things that diminish some elements of uncertainty. Those efforts you make while you're pregnant that favorably impact your child's health are but one example. If you are concerned about the quality of schooling that your child may get, you might look into which neighborhoods have the best schools and move there, or maybe get involved with schools and help improve them for your children and others. You can often hedge against the risks associated with some uncertainty, so that if a bad outcome occurs, its impact on you is lessened through insurance in some form. You can't know what the tuition and other costs may be for the schooling your child may want to get later, so setting aside some money, in a protected account that avoids some taxes, may be a smart early move. Since much of those big unknowns about the state of the world affect most everyone, there's no simple insurance you can buy to protect yourself from them.

On the brighter side, some of that uncertainty is actually sort of fun, as for instance whether you'll have a boy or a girl, or just what your child's personality and interests and skills will be as she goes through her life.

In general, learning about how specific outcomes may affect you and your family and taking prudent steps to avoid the bad things and being prepared to take advantage of the opportunities that come along are always pretty good strategies. So give your child a sense of her potential and provide her with the motivation to take on the world in ways that are healthy, attractive to her, and that make a contribution. That's something you can do, and it may help both your child and the rest of the world just a bit.

EXTERNALITIES

There's an important concept that hasn't come up yet in our discussions of other choices, but which is relevant in thinking about having children. It is the concept of an *externality*, which is something that results from your action that affects others, often inadvertently or even unknowingly, or vice versa, something someone else does that has an effect on you.

There are externalities all over the place—from the noise the teenager next door sends your way when he plays his drums loudly, to the attractive landscaping and shrubbery that your neighbor planted and cares for that you enjoy when you walk around the block, to congestion on the road that's imposed by each of us on the rest of us as we drive our cars, especially during rush hours. Some externalities are good while some are bad; they are often unintended but sometimes purposely disregarded when they are costly to avoid and a by-product of some other attractive activity. Driving your car and burning gasoline that emits carbon dioxide that fouls the air is a well-known negative externality that most of us impose on one another.

So what's the reason this comes up here? Well, children—yes, your child—imposes lots of externalities on everyone else in your community. Some are good and some aren't. In the years to come your child will likely (hopefully) bring a lot of joy and good experiences to your friends and neighbors, and his work may be influential, well beyond his salary or reputation, in improving the lives of many people. Just being a productive member of society in the decades ahead— with a work product that others want to have and a salary that gives him some security and your community some needed tax revenue has a lot of "positive externality." But then he'll also take some space and need some public schooling that will cost your neighbors. He, like everyone else, will impose some congestion here or there. Clearly then, your private decision about having children will have some externalities. Your decision will impose some costs and some benefits on your neighbors. Mostly, they will be positive, and perhaps that's one reason there will be some genuine happiness all around when you have your child.

As you might expect, there are several ways that society has come up with to deal with externalities. Probably the worst way is the one we employ most often—we ignore them. If you think about it, it would be sensible to encourage all of us to do more of the things that result in positive externalities, those that we enjoy or find beneficial. Similarly, we should discourage all of us from doing the things that have negative externalities. When we just ignore them, we get too much of the negative ones and too few of the positive ones. So how do we, collectively, influence people? Sometimes by focusing on the externality itself and either imposing a cost on us when we produce a negative one or giving some award for producing more of the good ones. For example, it is a serious negative externality when we violate traffic laws and run red lights or drive fast past local schools. We're all familiar with the costs imposed on us when we produce one of these negative externalities (and get caught). The same might be done by imposing a fee on us when we use gasoline in our car and thereby release noxious chemicals into the air, or perhaps your community has a higher fee for using the toll roads during rush hours as a way of charging for the congestion externality. Those fees encourage behaviors from which we all benefit. Similarly, one reason we have prestigious prizes for excellence in writing poetry or literature or for scientific discoveries is that those prizes partly reflect the fact of the positive externality and encourage that behavior. That's one reason for patents when someone invents something useful. It gives the inventor a little extra, over and above what he earns from his invention, a bit of "monopoly power" for a few years. The rationale is that this encourages inventions and their positive externalities.

When it comes to your child, society benefits from your having and raising a child. So it makes sense that there would be some social benefits from doing so—some acknowledgment of the positive externalities that encourages you to have that child. These include the public outlays that reduce your personal cost of having a child, like public schools and income tax advantages. Some societies have concluded that they would like their citizens to have more children, so they engage in "pro-natalist" policies intended to encourage fertility. These policies can include paid maternity and paternity leave from work while the child is young, subsidized child care for preschoolers, and bigger tax breaks for parents with more kids. These reflect the sense of positive benefits to all of society from the action that parents take to bear and rear children.

The fact of externalities from your child can explain why society at large has a stake in your private decision about your own fertility. But the argument that externalities exist, and what they are, can be used to promote more social intervention than some feel warranted, as we'll see in the next section.

PRINCIPAL-AGENT

There's another concept that we might put on the table at this point. The notion is that of a *principal-agent* relationship. There are lots of instances of this in our lives, circumstances in which we have someone who acts as our supervisor, guide, or negotiator—our "agent." You are likely to *be* the agent yourself for some folks, perhaps your aging parents who can no longer make sensible decisions because of cognitive impairment. If you are their agent, they are the principal, the persons for whom you act as agent.

That notion is also the way to think about owning a share of stock: when you own a piece of the firm, you are the principal, the owner, but you probably don't know how to run the company and cannot be in on all the decisions involving its actions, so there are managers who act as your agent in making those corporate decisions. That's why CEOs are always talking about making decisions on behalf of their shareholders. They are acting as the agent for those shareholders—at least that's the idea.

Well, when it comes to your children, you are clearly their agent. A young child isn't capable of making her own decisions about many important things, from picking up a hot skillet to not walking too close to the edge of a swimming pool. You are her agent; she is the principal. At one level this is just another way to talk about parenting. But it offers us a few insights.

If you have children, one of the more perplexing decisions you'll probably face is when to exercise your role as your child's agent, and when to allow or to encourage your child to act on her own behalf. Early on there's not a lot of ambiguity, as your child needs you to guide her, protect her, stimulate her, and teach her. But as she grows, the circumstances arise when she can do some of these tasks for herself, but not as well as you can do them for her. So what's the right choice then?

At some point you'll want her to learn to act on her own and be independent, but is that when another child takes her toy, or when her teacher asks a bit too much of her, or when her sports coach doesn't give her what seems like a fair shot in the game? The principal-agent relationship you as a parent have with your child is one of the more demanding but rewarding challenges you'll probably face as a parent.

There's another principal-agent relationship you'll have as a parent, and it too can be important. As the overseer of your child, you have the authority, the sovereignty, to make decisions on your child's behalf. Don't overlook the fact that there is expertise out there in the form of counselors and advisers who can give you information about what might be best for your child. Often you'll benefit from someone else's assessment of what's best for your child—those advisers are acting as your agent as you act as principal, deciding what to do for your child. Don't confuse being your child's adviser, guide, and nurturer with having to make each decision on your own. You, too, can benefit from advice. You can be both agent for your child and principal with your own adviser or agent.

A principal-agent relationship comes up in yet another circumstance that is fraught with controversy. There are times when the government acts as the agent for your child. That can be fine in lots of cases, but at times it can conflict with parents' sense of their right to be the child's agent. A couple examples clarify the notion and the conflicts here.

Our society has laws that stipulate that your child must be enrolled in school (well, there are provisions for home-schooling, but let's put that aside). There are a couple reasons for those laws, and most adults agree with both of them: first, your child has a right to be educated, and, second, the community collectively has a right to have your child educated. The first notion asserts that the child has a right to be educated whether the parent agrees or not. That's an example of the state acting as the child's agent, even overriding the parent's rights. The parent must send the child to school at least through the grades that take him up to age 16.

The other notion has more to do with what's good for the community: it has to do with those externalities. For the community to function well, it is important that everyone be educated—everyone needs to be able to read, to do enough math to engage in commerce in the community, et cetera, so again the community has collectively decided to have laws that children must be educated. The state, or society at large, is the agent for us all collectively in this case, again overriding the parent's agency. So far, so good, since we mostly all agree on these two points about schooling all our children.

Another example begins with the recognition of externality from infectious diseases that can be prevented by vaccination. Here the state steps in and mandates that children be vaccinated. The state is acting as our agent, protecting us all from the risk of those diseases. But if a parent, for whatever reason, wishes to avoid vaccinating the child, there is a conflict between the legitimate agency of the state to protect us all and that of the parent to make decisions on behalf of the child.

To resolve this would take us way beyond the choices we are focused on in this little book. To see that it requires a few principles to guide that judgment, notice that we would all, probably, agree that the government has the right to set the law that cars must stop at red traffic lights, and a parent has no right to give her child permission to disregard that law. Then, too, we would all, probably, agree that the government does not have the right to require that children eat broccoli once a week. There, a parent's right to decide is dominant. Cases in between define the edges of who has what rights. Parents' rights matter most, except in certain cases where there's a clear reason why the state may step in.

Another difficult example is when the state determines that the parent is harming or abusing the child. Then, in what's a most complex and difficult circumstance, the government can declare itself a better agent for the child. It can take the extreme step of removing the child from the parent's care. We would probably all agree that there are some instances of extreme abuse in which this state action is warranted. But there are always boundary disputes about this—what level of parental inattention, parental selfishness, or physical punishing as discipline constitutes abuse that justifies state intervention?

Communities differ in their answers, as you might expect. There isn't a clear right answer that we all agree upon in all circumstances. That's why it useful to understand the notion of principal-agent relationships and to look into what the justification is for overriding parental agency of their children. A claim of externality can be that justification, but it can easily be asserted when it isn't really a strong case. It's a judgment, a choice you'll need to make as an informed citizen, but one that's a bit beyond our topic here.

THE 1980S COHORT'S FERTILITY

By ages 25–29, some 41% of those in the 1980s Cohort—born in 1980–1984—had had at least one child, as we see in table 5.3. Well more than half of blacks had done so. As to the timing of the first birth, almost 11% overall had a child before turning 18. Of those with a child, the early twenties was the time in life when about half of each group had their first child. Interestingly, that is true for both the men and the women, although a much larger percentage of the women had begun having children before age 20.

Table 5.4 shows the number of children this cohort had by age 20 (panel A) and by age 25 (panel B). We see that, overall, about one in five (18.3%) had at least one child by age 20, and about one in three (35.3%) had done so by age 25. For the men, by age 25 only one in ten had more than one child, but the proportion with at least one had grown a lot in the preceding five years. As we look at table 5.4, it is good to remind ourselves that these women have at least an additional 15 years of potential childbearing and the men have even more, so the pattern of childbearing here reflects only the early stages of the cohort's ultimate fertility. If you are in your twenties, however, the pattern of early childbearing may be the most interesting for you to compare with your own and your friends' pattern of having children.

There is a lot we can do to look at the linkages between several of the choices we've been discussing. We can look at fertility by marital status, for example. Table 5.5 shows the number of children born by age 20 and by age 25 by age at first marriage. In general, those who married earlier began having their children at a much younger age. By age 25 they also have had considerably more children. But, then, of those who had not yet married by age 25 (panel B), 10% had had two or more children. While there has been a steady rise in nonmarital childbearing in the United States over the past few decades, there is still a pretty close link between the timing of formal mar-

Table 5.3: Having Children

	Population	Whites	Blacks	Hispanics	Females	Males
Panel A: Percentage Who Have Had a Child (by 2009)						
Had a child	41.0%	35.6%	57.9%	50.2%	47.5%	34.8%
Panel B: Age at First Birth (of those who have had a child)						
Age						
13–15	2.0%	1.0%	4.5%	2.3%	2.4%	1.4%
16–17	8.6	6.6	12.1	10.7	11.3	5.2
18–19	17.5	16.3	19.7	19.7	20.0	14.2
20–24	49.0	48.6	48.9	50.7	47.2	51.4
25–29	22.9	27.5	14.8	16.6	18.9	27.8

Source: The 1980s Cohort.

Table 5.4: Number of Children by Age 20 and by Age 25

	Population	Whites	Blacks	Hispanics	Females	Males
Panel A: Number of Children by Age 20						
None	81.7%	85.7%	69.4%	74.7%	75.2%	87.8%
1	14.8	11.8	23.8	20.1	19.5	10.3
2	3.1	2.3	5.8	4.4	4.7	1.7
3	0.4	0.2	0.7	0.8	0.6	0.2
4–6	0.0	0.0	0.2	0.0	0.0	0.0
Panel B: Number of Children by Age 25						
None	64.7%	70.4%	47.6%	54.6%	58.3%	70.8%
1	19.6	17.5	26.3	22.8	20.5	18.6
2	10.4	8.4	16.0	14.8	13.8	7.3
3	3.9	2.9	7.0	6.1	5.3	2.6
4–8	1.3	0.8	3.1	1.7	2.0	0.6

Source: The 1980s Cohort.

riage and both the timing and the number of children born. The men and women in this 1980s group reflect that pattern.

You'll notice a vertical line in each of the two panels of table 5.5. It alerts us to the fact that those to its right had not yet (if ever) married by the time they first had a child. That is, panel A shows that of those who married at ages 20–24, while 73% of them had no children when they turned 20, some 22% of them already had one child by age 20 before they married, and some 4% of them had two children. The far right-hand column in each of the two panels shows the fertility for

Table 5.5: Number of Children by Whether Married and by Age at First Marriage

| | Age at First Marriage | | | | |
No. of Children	by 17	18–19	20–24	25–29	Never Married
Panel A: Number of Children by Age 20					
None	22%	34%	73%	90%	86%
1	39	46	22	8	12
2	28	17	4	2	2
3	12	3	0	0	0
Panel B: Number of Children by Age 25					
None	14%	19%	36%	70%	76%
1	6	26	34	21	15
2	41	35	22	6	6
3	26	15	6	2	3
4	10	4	2	1	1
5+	3	2	0	0	0

Source: The 1980s Cohort.

those who had not ever married: 14% had a child by age 20, and 24% had done so by age 25.

Table 5.6 shows us that there is a strong connection between the 1980s Cohort's family background and their fertility by their late twenties. Table 5.6 focuses on the 1980s Cohort's father's education, mother's age at her first birth, the family structure when the Cohort member was age 14, and the family's poverty status at that age. All four are closely linked to the Cohort member's fertility. Look at the left-hand column showing the percentage of the Cohort who had a child: well over half of those whose father had less than 12 years of education had a child but less than a quarter of those whose father had 16 or more years of education had a child by the ages 25–29. Those with less-educated fathers began having their children earlier and have had substantially more children.

Similarly, there's a strong connection between their mother's age at her first birth and the Cohort member's own fertility. Again, the connection is strong between growing up in an intact family or with a single parent and the Cohort member's own fertility by the late twenties. And, finally, that same qualitative linkage is seen for those who grew up in poverty or well above.

The behavior of their parents and the circumstances in which they

Table 5.6: Relationship of Family Background and the Timing and Number of Children (row percentages for each outcome)

	Have Had a Child	Age at First Birth				Number of Children by Age 25			
		< 17	17–19	20–24	25–29	0	1	2	3+
Panel A: Father's Education Level									
> 12 years	55%	6%	25%	52%	16%	51%	24%	17%	8%
12 years	45	5	21	50	24	62	22	11	5
13–15 years	35	3	17	49	31	71	19	7	3
16+ years	22	2	16	44	37	82	13	4	1
Panel B: Mother's Age at First Birth									
> 18	65%	9%	30%	47%	13%	41%	28%	18%	13%
18–19	56	7	28	51	14	50	25	16	9
20–30	37	4	20	49	27	68	18	9	4
31+	25	5	19	48	29	79	13	5	3
Panel C: Family Structure at Age 14									
Family intact	31%	3%	16%	50%	31%	74%	17%	7%	2%
Divorced	46	6	23	50	20	60	22	11	7
Single parent	56	10	32	43	15	51	23	16	10
Other	51	5	26	49	19	55	23	14	8
Panel D: Family Poverty Status at Age 14									
In poverty	58%	9%	29%	47%	14%	48%	23%	17%	12%
Slightly above poverty	44	4	23	52	21	61	22	12	5
> two times their poverty level	31	3	16	48	33	75	17	6	2

*Ratio of family income to family poverty threshold less than 1.0, between 1.0 and 2.0, or above 2.0, respectively.
Source: The 1980s Cohort.

grew up are, evidently, closely linked to the fertility choices those in the 1980s Cohort made. Table 5.6 shows us that's true for the choice about the age at first birth and the number of children they have had so far. We can't say that the family background is the reason for the Cohort member's choices, but we can say that the parental choices are definitely reflected in the choices made by their children, our 1980s Cohort.

If that was true for these parents who made their choices in the 1960s and 1970s and their children's choices made in the 1990s and 2000s, it is probably also going to be true that your own children's behaviors will be influenced by the choices you make. Like so much in life, you can look at that as good news or bad news. If you make good choices that are helpful and healthy ones for you personally, those choices may have a pretty big influence on your children's life. That's the good news. Of course, the other side of that coin is that if you make poor choices, they can also influence your children. While the theme throughout this book is that the choices are yours to make, table 5.6 suggests that your decisions have an influence on others whom you will likely care a lot about in the years to come.

PARENTING

When it comes to adult choices, none is more impactful than the decision to have a child. In recent years fewer men and women have chosen to have children, and many have chosen to have somewhat fewer. The cost of bearing and rearing a child is one reason for this. As we've discussed, much of that cost is an opportunity cost of the parent's time. We've seen that more educated men and women have higher wage rates, so the opportunity cost of their time is greater. Since they face a higher cost for having a child, those more educated people tend to have fewer children.

We focused on some of what's known about the choice of spending time and other resources on your kids, emphasizing a couple points. First, it seems that making a big effort early in your child's life is really important for the child's later development and success. That goes right down to some of the things the mom does while she is pregnant, and probably nothing she does later has more impact on her child than her avoiding alcohol, tobacco, and drugs during that crucial time. After the birth, the more time spent with the child seems to be really important, talking to the child, engaging with his interests, helping him understand how the world works, and giving him a sense of his own worth and efficacy.

We noted that there's this matter of emphasizing the present or the future in the choice about having children. We also acknowledged the considerable uncertainty associated with having and raising a child. Then there were a couple new concepts that haven't come up in the previous chapters. One is the notion of *externalities* since your personal decision about having children and how you raise your kids has influence on your neighbors and your community. Another is the idea of *principal-agency* where you act on behalf of your child, at least while she's little, and then you must make some choices about when and how to relax your agency and allow your child to begin to make her own choices. Lots here, but then this is a really big deal, and the fact that you can get into the parenting business without even choosing to do so is itself one of the considerations you'll have to make some decisions about.

SIX | Health Habits

Early to bed and early to rise, makes a man healthy . . .

BEN FRANKLIN

Health is one of those things that if you have it in abundance, you hardly notice it at all—if your health is good, it isn't a particularly important part of your conscious life. If you have poor health, however, and especially if you suffer serious impairment, it becomes a major factor in your daily life. It can dramatically alter your long-term plans and capabilities.

Probably no one you know would choose to have bad health, so in a book about making choices, it may seem odd to focus on health. But like so many of the other decisions we face, health has lots of dimensions, as well as some close linkages to some of the other big choices we've already discussed. Some of the factors that determine our health are clearly within our control; some are not. Some factors are unique to each of us while some are community-wide. And some factors are purely random. But despite the reality that there's a lot of pure chance in what diseases we contract, what ailments we confront, or what accidents we endure, there are many decisions we make that influence our health.

One thing you do to improve your health is buy products—from aspirin for your headaches to glasses for your eyesight—and from time to time you buy some expert guidance and treatment from your doctor. You also spend some of your own time on behalf of your health, exercising, waiting to see the doctor, and lying in bed as your body heals itself from an infection or an accident or an operation.

As if you were the CEO of a little firm that produces your own health, you use goods and services that you buy, some of your time, and some of your entrepreneurial skills as you organize your effort to overcome impairments. You also produce a base health status to ward off disease, to keep yourself fit, and to look good and feel healthy and energetic. The things you do to sustain your health probably include exercise, maybe watching your diet, brushing your teeth, and on and on.

And while there are lots of things people do to protect and to enhance their health, there is another whole group of behaviors that can harm your health. We all do some of these, and we can't avoid some of them, like riding in a car. We choose to engage in sports that have high rates of accidents. Then there are things we know are quite unhealthy, and even though we don't have to do them, we choose to do them anyway, because they have some other attractive feature.

Some behaviors, like smoking, involve long-term, cumulative effects on your health. Others, like bungee jumping, involve one-time risks that either impact you or don't. While you may not have thought about it this way, the whole array of these activities reveal your attitude toward your health and the priority you place on having and maintaining good health. What you do routinely that affects your health, either positively or negatively, constitutes your *health habits*. That's the life choice we'll discuss in this chapter.

HEALTH PRODUCTION AND SCARCITY

Choices arise because you can't have it both ways; you face scarcity. Suppose you made a list of the things you could do that would be beneficial to your health and another list of things you could do that would be potentially harmful to your health. Some of the items on the first list might not seem very appealing, just healthy, like watching your diet. You have to decide how much you're going to pay attention to this, and you'll either avoid eating too much of those tasty but unhealthy things, or not. It's a choice.

Similarly, there are some things on the second list that may seem pretty appealing, like driving home after having some drinks instead of paying for a taxi or maybe skydiving. Again, you have to choose— in every case, of course, you can't both do it and not do it. You either run the risk or miss the fun. It's your choice, but a choice it is.

What makes these choices about your health even more important is that they can become habits. Habits are handy. Without them, we would face many situations every day that would make us think through every choice we want to make. If we establish habits that reflect our judgments, values, and interests, we don't have to take time, each instance, to make a decision—we just react, based on a habit. Sure, we can tweak the habit or consciously override it now and then, but a well-developed habit guides a lot of what we do and say.

We probably have a few habits that we wish we didn't have, and we may be pretty proud of some other habits. Some can reflect our honesty or integrity, our inquisitiveness or curiosity, or our compassion for others, and others reflect our inclination to be self-protective or self-promotional.

Since you face all sorts of choices every day and in so many diverse circumstances, you inevitably already have basic strategies for most things, just so you don't have to ponder each one, every time. The general strategies that you adopt for yourself regarding your health are your health habits. And when you consciously consider the types of health habits you adopt, that is where the decision comes in.

Some people adopt pretty cautious, healthy habits, and they miss out on some attractive things. Others adopt a more carefree strategy, living more on the edge, which may be exciting but risks some pretty serious health detriments. There's a lot in between, not so risky but not too bland. Your choice.

I've got a friend who knows a lot about cuts and bruises and how to bandage himself effectively. His lifestyle puts him at risk so he has a need to know. It's because he is an avid cyclist and inevitably gets into an accident now and then. He takes those risks because the bike gives him a lot of satisfaction. He chooses to put up with those bruises and scrapes as one of the costs of his sport. On the other hand, he doesn't completely ignore the risks, either. For example, he doesn't ride too close to other cyclists in fast team rides, he always wears a helmet, and he knows how to take care of those cuts and bruises.

Depending on what sorts of things give you pleasure, and whether or not risk itself is something you enjoy, there are lots of different strategies for "producing" your own good health. Some people are particularly cautious and avoid risks; others are not so cautious but very efficient in addressing health problems when they arise. Some people are aware of particular risks that they face because of their genes or family history; others know they put themselves at risk by the occupation they've chosen, or the location of their house, or some other important choice they've made.

No one can make a health-enhancing choice every time. And even if we did, there's a lot of pure chance, just random bad luck, in what health issues arise. So no matter how cautious you are, you'll always be making choices that can influence your health and will be engaged in efforts to remedy one or another health problem. You, the CEO of your little health-production endeavor, will be busy throughout your lifetime.

Whatever choices you make or habits you form, you will need to learn to deal with your health problems, both in avoiding some and fixing others. There are skills involved and attitudes about how carefully you'll follow your physician's guidance. And just like other skills—from cooking to singing to speaking a foreign language to kayaking—these skills accumulate. If you make a conscious effort to become good at caring for your health, those skills and the associated habits become both easier and more natural to you.

When you have a partner and children, your habits impact them, as well. Your own choices about health habits spill over to those you love. This, incidentally, is another of those *externalities*, where your decisions about your own health have an impact, good or bad, on others. You know that's so for something like secondhand smoke. But it's also true with many of your habits of caution, your conscious decisions about diet and exercise, about following the advice of medical experts, and about a lot of the ways in which you live.

It is well known (and documented) that people who are married tend to be in better health and live longer. The two of you policing one another a bit, nudging yourselves in the direction of health-enhancing actions, and having two heads to think through how best to deal with a health problem, all impact your health and the health of those with whom you live.

HEALTH AS AN ASSET

When you count your blessings or list your assets, your health is key. Just as your schooling gives you skills, knowledge, certification, and

Table 6.1: Life Expectancy at Age 25, by Education Level and
Gender, 2006

| Education Level | Years of Expected Life Remaining at Age 25 | |
	Females	Males
No high school diploma	52	47
High school graduate or GED	57	51
Some college	58	52
Bachelor's degree or higher	60	56

Source: National Center for Health Statistics, Health, United States, 2011:
Special Feature on Socioeconomic Status and Health: Adults, fig. 32: "Life
Expectancy at Age 25, by Sex and Education Level: United States, 1996 and
2006," http://www.cdc.gov/nchs/data/hus/2011/fig32.pdf.

self-confidence that help you in your job and in your "productive"
activities at home, your health gives you capability. Since you spend
money, time, effort, and energy to maintain or improve your health,
it doesn't take a big stretch of the imagination to see your health as
an asset, another part of your *human capital*.

In fact, there is a lot of evidence that these two forms of human
capital, education and health, have a pretty strong relationship. Table
6.1, for instance, shows how much longer 25-year-olds with different
levels of education are expected to live. For females, a 25-year-old
who hadn't completed high school can expect to live, on average, 52
more years. Those who had graduated from high school could expect
to live an additional 5 years, however. And those with a college degree could expect to live 3 years beyond that, all based on the actual
pattern of deaths by level of education. Table 6.1 shows a similar pattern for males.[1]

There are several good reasons for this strong positive relationship between schooling and health, and there's been a lot of research on this subject.[2] For one thing, having more schooling and
being more productive with your time probably means that you are
also more productive in taking care of your health. That is, those with
more schooling are more efficient in their health-care purchases
and with the time needed to help generate their good health. They
likely have better health habits and are more knowledgeable about
protecting their health. In short, schooling helps people produce
their own good health.

And that's only one reason. Another is that to get the job and earn the higher salary that schooling enables, one needs to be reasonably healthy, so the incentive to be in good health is higher for those with more education. A third factor is the issue we've discussed several times already—time preference.

If a guy's time preference dramatically favors the present, he isn't as likely to value the advantage of making a big investment in his education or in his health. He will live for today, have lots of fun, and not worry much about his own future, since, by definition, he doesn't care so much about his future. People with a strong preference for today—with a high "discount rate" on the future—will make the decision not to invest in either schooling or health.

Those with a weaker preference for the present—with a lower discount rate on the future—will likely make a bigger investment in schooling and skills, and will also make a bigger effort to maintain their health. The difference among people in their time preference can account for some of the positive association between education level and health.

There are in fact many factors that affect both education choices and health habit choices in the same way. These include the culture of one's family, personal aspirations, lifestyle, and responsibilities. That is, families differ in the emphasis they place on things like schooling. You'll see this in stories about families from different ethnicities or different regions of the world. Families that encourage their children to invest heavily in schooling also tend to encourage habits that enhance health.

In a similar vein, people differ in what they aspire to accomplish in their lifetime. Those who have grand aspirations will tend to make the sort of efforts in schooling and in caring for their own health that will enable them to achieve those aspirations. These sorts of differences among people can also lead to a positive relationship between education and health—those who invest heavily in schooling do so in their health as well.

Additionally, while your health helps you earn more and protects the investment you've made in your education, it also carries over to affect the well-being of your loved ones. If it resonated with you and you thought it sounded correct that there is a family "culture"—that is, things one family values or emphasizes in its routines that carry over from generation to generation—then it should also be apparent to you that you are a model for your children. How you treat your health is likely to influence how they treat their own. This is one of many examples of the effects that your health choices will have on others. Let's take a look at other ways this can happen.

EXTERNALITIES

As discussed in chapter 5, any consequence of something you do that has an impact on others, often unintentionally or indirectly, is called an externality. For example, if you have a child, this impacts others. These externalities can be good or bad. In addition to the ways in which your health habits affect those in your family, as mentioned above, there are lots of other externalities in this area.

Let's consider a big one, which is also mentioned in chapter 5 on children: vaccinations. There are, currently, some sixteen diseases that can be prevented by a vaccination. These include a bunch of pretty awful sicknesses, including chicken pox, diphtheria, Hepatitis A and B, HPV, measles, mumps, polio, tetanus, whooping cough, and others.

Whooping cough, for example, is highly contagious and can be spread when someone with the pertussis bacteria coughs or sneezes close to you. In 2012 there were over 41,000 cases of whooping cough in the United States, and fortunately only a few deaths caused by the disease.[3] Whooping cough makes breathing difficult and is very uncomfortable; it is far more dangerous in small infants, causing life-threatening lapses in breathing. Apparently protection from this vaccine decreases over time, so teenagers or adults need a revaccination.

For our discussion, the point is that if everyone you encounter in the course of your day has been vaccinated against these terrible diseases, your chance of contracting one of them is pretty low. But if in your community there isn't much vaccination, then it is a lot more likely that you will run into and contract one of these diseases. So if people in your community get vaccinated, that is a positive externality for you. And it's just as true that you impose a positive externality on the people you meet if you have been vaccinated. That's why schools have requirements about vaccinations, so their students are less likely to contract one of these diseases from classmates. It's why there are often public service campaigns to urge flu shots to reduce the risk of a contagious disease like influenza.

A major scourge on society in earlier times was caused by a highly contagious virus: smallpox, which causes an extensive rash and a high fever. At one time it had a fatality rate of about 30%, and among those who survived, it often left many lifetime scars on the body, especially on the face. Because of widespread vaccination, however, smallpox was eliminated in the United States soon after World War II. And according to the Centers for Disease Control and Prevention, the last "naturally occurring case in the world was in Somalia in 1977."[4] So that's one disease that vaccination has wiped out—and a good thing, too, since there was no known treatment.

We no longer even need a vaccine against that disease. If you want to think of it this way, our grandparents and their generation gave us today a big positive externality in the form of removing the risk of that disease through their choice of getting vaccinated.

So when you get vaccinated against the flu, you lower your own risk of getting that illness and you impose a positive externality on others. They do the same for you when they get vaccinated. There are lots of these health-related externalities, some positive, like vaccinations, and some negative. One that you'll want to think about is the risk of diseases that are transmitted by sexual contact. Here, again, there are some pretty nasty diseases, as discussed in chapter 4. Most of these aren't controlled by vaccination. But there are other things you can do to avoid getting these diseases, and as is the case with any communicable disease, if you avoid getting the disease, you avoid giving it to anyone else, so you impose a positive externality on them as well as a clear benefit to yourself.

In the case of these STDs, the best way to avoid contracting them is to avoid having sex with someone who has one of them. That, however, isn't always easy to do, since you usually can't look at someone and know if he or she is infectious. You can ask, and if your sex partner cares about you, perhaps he or she will tell you so—if he or she knows. A couple strategies for dealing with this risk are pretty well known: avoid having sex with people you don't know awfully well or don't care a lot about, and don't have sex with very many people, as was shown vividly in table 4.4. One sex partner only is most effective in preventing disease transmission if both of you only partner with one another. Of course total abstinence works even better, but the downside of that is pretty obvious and not all that appealing to most adults.

The other strategy is to use protection, that is, a physical barrier to the transmission of the fluids that pass the virus or bacteria. The one that's most available and works well is a condom. While this can be motivated by your own eagerness to avoid getting a disease, it also provides the positive externality for your partner (and, yes, it also helps prevent pregnancy at the same time).

So, health-promoting habits like getting vaccinated and using a condom during risky sex are examples of positive externalities in the health area. There are also negative ones. If you smoke, you expose those with whom you spend a lot of time to the risks of secondhand smoke, a negative externality. For another, your health habits are seen by those you love (including your children), and your choices provide guidance for them. You may be a role model, so here the externality may be positive or negative depending on your behavior.

There's also a more subtle externality that's too often overlooked. By protecting your own health, you have a positive effect on your loved ones since they have concerns about your health and they face distress and anxiety if you are unhealthy. They may also suffer a lot of inconvenience when you are ill or unable to do what you normally can do. If your earnings fall because of an illness or accident you might have avoided, your loved ones suffer the consequences along with you. These are all externalities.

More broadly, your health habits impact the wider community through other externalities. Your community incurs a lot of public health costs in efforts to lower health risks and prevent diseases. Community hospitals and subsidies large and small are paid for by taxes or fees. Your community bears all sorts of indirect costs to pay for your health. You may suffer an accident or come down with a disease that enables you to claim disability support while you are ill, for example. Some of those costs are covered by your own insurance perhaps, but some may be paid by the company you work for if your condition impacts its insurance rates, and some may be paid by tax-payers, if it is public support you benefit from.

It's most likely a good thing that we have these humane and car-ing institutions and practices that help all of us at times. But, still, if you choose to put yourself at risk of an accident or a disease, your action imposes a negative externality on your neighbors, just as their choices can impose the same externalities on you.

UNCERTAINTY

There's surely a lot of uncertainty surrounding your health. There's the uncertainty about an illness or something that incapacitates you; there's the risk of an accident. There are uncertainties about just what sort of health care you'll need and when you'll need it and for how long. And of course there's uncertainty about the finality of your life itself. It's a morbid topic, but one that's important to think about. It's better to face up to some of the choices you will make, one way or an-other, than to ignore them and confront your health problems when something happens.

As I've said in previous chapters, there are three things one can do about an uncertainty: (1) you can come to understand and assess it; (2) you can often do things to lower the chances of bad things hap-pening; and (3) you can usually take steps to lower the adverse effects of the bad thing if it does happen. My cyclist friend who I mentioned above has done what one should do with a risk: he has assessed it and understands what's involved (by knowing he will occasionally be in an accident); he has taken steps to lower the risks (by not riding too close to other riders); and he has done things to offset the dam-ages if and when an accident occurs (by wearing a helmet and being able to attend to minor injuries).

Other uncertainties about health offer great examples of why all three of these strategies make sense. Let's take them one by one. Understanding how a health setback can affect your work and your family life was central in our earlier discussion about the linkage between your education and your health. If your health fails you, all the knowledge and skill in the world won't add up to much, as you are unable to make use of them because you're ill or incapacitated. So you will probably want to do what you can to keep your health in good shape, if only to be able to make the best use of the schooling you've had.

If you have a physician you visit from time to time, it's likely he or she has asked you about the health history of your parents and siblings and maybe your grandparents. There's a message in those questions: you have inherited a lot of the same genes as those family members, so their experiences, for some types of health outcomes, can indicate something about your risk of one disease or another. To assess and understand the risks you face, you might want to talk with your family members about the health histories of your recent ancestors, how and at what age your grandparents died if they are deceased, and what illnesses they've had along the way.

Knowing your family's health history gives you some basis for anticipating what your own health may be like as the years go by. The information provides an indication of what's likely, but not more than that—much of your health depends on you, and much of it is just random luck, good or bad, so don't get too hung up on those family histories. You can reduce the uncertainty here, but you can't eliminate it.

The second element of a sensible strategy on health uncertainty is to do what you can to stay in good health. Here, there's a lot of room for action, which can have a big effect. We can spend a lot of money and time either doing what we can to avoid health problems or fixing our health after it fails. The efforts and expenditures focused on keeping your health in good shape don't get nearly as much attention in advertisements or public promotion as do the expenditures to fix every little health problem you might run into. There are big companies out there hoping to sell you goods and services to improve your health. There are fewer commercial benefit to firms, however, from convincing you to exercise, to eat the right sort of diet, and to avoid products that can harm your health.

Here's an interesting thing about all those expenditures on your health: of all the things you spend money on over the year, the only one that it would be ideal to spend nothing on is health care. If you had perfect health, you wouldn't need any of those products or services (on which the average U.S. household spent over $3,000 in 2010, or about 7% of their total spending—not including insurance costs).[5] Unlike what you spend on food or shelter or clothes or entertainment or most anything else, your medical care expenses are made to prevent or cure bad health. All the other items are things you enjoy having and give other things up for. But if your health were perfect and going to stay that way, your health expenditures would just disappear from your budget.

But, of course, your health is probably not perfect and is certainly not going to stay that way—you can't eliminate your risk of disease and all health problems. Those genes and the social and physical environment in which you live have their influence on your health, and then there's the random factor. Still, you can, by your own health habits, dramatically affect your health and your need to spend money and time fixing your health. And habits are things you just do. You get in a groove and don't need to think about habits a lot—that's what makes them habits.

So if you develop healthy habits when you are younger, you can save a lot of hassle, worry, discomfort, and probably a lot of money and time too. The choice here is more like the choice about schooling than you might have figured: one option is to make an effort and pay a cost of inconvenience, time, and some money now and get into a groove of healthy habits. Alternatively you can skip all that, not worry now, and thereby increase the risk of health problems later when you'll have to pay in money, time, probably inconvenience, and pain. That old present-future issue is raising its head here again.

The third strategy for dealing with uncertainty is to take steps to lower not the likelihood of it happening but the adverse effect on you if it does. The main technique here is insurance, which we've not addressed yet. Suppose there's a 1 in 1,000 chance that, say, your house burns down within the year, and it would cost you $300,000 to replace. That's an amount you really cannot come up with, so you'd be in deep trouble if it occurred. Now, if there are lots of people in just that same circumstance, facing that same low-probability but awful event, there's a much better strategy than just each one of you hoping you're not the unlucky one next year. If you and, say, 10,000 people who all face that same risk get together and everyone contributes $300 this year, an amount each of you can afford, then if 1 in 1,000 suffers the loss of their house, that will be 10 people out of the 10,000 in the insurance pool. The payments into the pool at $300 per household would be a total of $3 million—just what those 10 people need, at $300,000 each, to replace their home.

The 10 tragic fires protected by insurance with a large number of people all paying a "premium" that is "actuarially fair" means that no one is wiped out, and every household in the pool paid the same $300, faced the same risk, and ended up in the same condition (aside from the hassle and inconveniences of rebuilding). That's the way insurance works, simply put. There are lots of complications we could introduce, but you see how appealing this idea is—it shares the cost and removes the terrible risk that you might be wiped out financially if a bad event occurs to you. Pretty appealing, indeed.

The same principle applies to the risks you face from a major health problem. They can come up unexpectedly, without warning, and they can be devastatingly expensive. If you've done what you can to lower the risks of something bad happening, the other thing you can do is to insure yourself and your family against those devastating expenses.

You'll have some health-care expenses that are essentially protective or diagnostic and not really elements that involve risk, just expense. A dental cleaning, an annual physical checkup, and replacing your eyeglasses periodically are examples of expenses you'll have that aren't really "risks." Insuring against them doesn't make a lot of sense. It is the unexpected (and too often big) expense—the cancer that comes seemingly from nowhere and costs so much to address, or the heart attack or stroke that you never expected but now has happened and has all sorts of associated costs—these and many other health surprises are the things you'll want to insure against.

It really is unwise to live your life with these risks hanging over your head. In light of the uncertainty regarding your health, health insurance is really a must—not only for you but on behalf of those who love you, since if one of these health events befalls you, your family is likely to feel the need to pay as much as they can to help out, so getting that insurance is an act of love on their behalf. This is yet another externality.

Accidents and bad health events happen, and they can happen to any of us—don't fool yourself by thinking you're immune or lucky or whatever. Insurance against those big expenses should be considered essential. It's rather nice that a competitive insurance company will likely give you some credit for lowering your risks if you have good health habits. For example, if you are a non-smoker and don't do any sky-diving, your insurance premiums should be a bit lower, as if to thank you for doing what you can do to lower those risks.

THE 1980S COHORT'S HEALTH HABITS

Let's begin our look at the health habits of the 1980s Cohort by considering how their health is. At age 20 each respondent was asked, "In general, how is your health: Excellent, Very Good, Good, Fair, or Poor?" Table 6.2 gives us their answers. Most reported to be in quite good health—one-third in excellent health and another third in very good health. There is, happily, very little difference among the race/ethnic groups in their health status at this age. There is a bit more difference between the females and the males, as is usually found to be the case: females typically report themselves to be in less good health than do males, and they typically see a doctor more often (we don't know that about this cohort, but it is usually the case), but they do live longer than men.

The same table can be prepared for the health status at age 25, but there is so little difference from the pattern shown in table 6.2 that it isn't shown—over those five years the health levels have declined only a small amount.

Another indicator of their health that we can consider is whether they are overweight or not. If one is substantially overweight, this

Table 6.2: Health Status at Age 20

Health Status	Population	Whites	Blacks	Hispanics	Females	Males
Excellent	33%	33%	33%	32%	27%	38%
Very Good	36	37	32	34	38	35
Good	25	24	26	28	28	22
Fair	6	5	8	7	7	5
Poor	1	1	1	0	1	0

Source: The 1980s Cohort.

Table 6.3: Obesity at Ages 20 and 25

	Population	Whites	Blacks	Hispanics	Females	Males
Panel A: Obese at Age 20?						
Yes	14%	12%	20%	17%	14%	14%
No	86	88	80	83	86	86
Panel B: Obese at Age 25?						
Yes	23%	21%	30%	30%	24%	23%
No	77	79	70	70	76	77

Source: The 1980s Cohort.

often indicates a health problem later. A good way to measure this is by a "body mass index," or BMI, which takes into consideration your height and your weight.[6] Based on the 1980s Cohort's self-reported height and weight at age 20 and at age 25, table 6.3 shows us the percentage of the 1980s Cohort that is obese, that is, the percentage that has a BMI of 30.0 or higher.

While the self-reported health status in table 6.2 was impressively positive, the indication of health based on BMI in table 6.3 isn't so positive. Here, by age 20, 14% overall are obese, and as many as 20% of blacks are so. The figures are of even greater concern by age 25, when overall some 23% are obese, and for both blacks and Hispanics, it is as high as 30%. That's a lot of added weight in only five years! We should note that these measures are based on self-reported height and weight, and may be a bit different from a measure taken with scales and a tape measure in a doctor's office. It isn't likely, however, that a lot of these folks overstated their weight.

We can only speculate why the cohort's health status appears to be more positive when it is self-assessed than when it is measured a bit more objectively by their BMI. These are relatively young people who probably do feel relatively healthy but, as table 6.4 suggests, even at the age of 20, there is already a noticeable relationship between their self-reported health status and obesity. For the population overall, of those who consider their health excellent only 8.3% are obese. However, the percentage of people who are obese rises as their reported health status declines; and for those who report themselves to be in poor health, 29% are obese. The relationship holds for all the subgroups shown in the table.

Table 6.4: Obesity by Health Status at Age 20

Health Status at 20	Population	Whites	Blacks	Hispanics	Females	Males
Excellent	8.3%	6.9%	13.1%	9.3%	7.6%	8.7%
Very good	12.6	10.6	18.4	15.6	11.2	14.0
Good	20.5	18.2	26.6	23.5	20.6	20.3
Fair	26.0	20.9	33.4	39.5	27.8	23.8
Poor	29.0	—*	—*	—*	30.4	—*

*Too few to calculate with precision.
Source: The 1980s Cohort.

Let's consider a few behaviors that influence health. One of the most frequent bits of advice about living a healthy life is to exercise routinely and to watch your diet. Another, of course, is to avoid doing things known to be unhealthy, like smoking, doing drugs, or drinking excessive amounts of alcohol. What's the story for the 1980s Cohort in terms of these health-related behaviors? Can we see signs that their behaviors have become health habits?

Table 6.5 provides some answers. A majority of the cohort reported that they didn't smoke, and that's the case for all the groups shown. Yet 40% did smoke, and of those who did, most reported doing so every day. The question asked was, "In the past 30 days, on how many days did you smoke a cigarette?" Overall, while 59% said zero, 29% said 20 or more. In fact, in detail not shown in the table, 24% said all 30 days, so a majority of those who reported smoking said they did so daily. Blacks reported relatively low levels of smoking, you'll notice.

Then there's diet. Panels B and C of the same table show how often those in the 1980s Cohort said they eat fruit (other than fruit juice) and vegetables (not counting French fries or potato chips). Veggies seem to be more popular than fruit with these folks, and there are not big differences among the subgroups here. Few report never having a piece of fruit or a vegetable (in the past month), and a quarter to a third report having fruits and vegetables daily. How about you?

And exercise. Panel D shows that at age 20, close to one-third (29%) of the 18 million men and women in the 1980s Cohort did not exercise for 30 minutes or more over the course of a week. Some 14%, on the other hand, reported that they did so about every day. Here, too, there isn't a big difference among the subgroups, except that the females reported somewhat less exercising than did the males.

Table 6.5: Unhealthy and Healthy Behaviors at Age 20

Frequency	Population	Whites	Blacks	Hispanics	Females	Males
Panel A: Smoking at Age 20 (days/month)						
None	59%	55%	71%	68%	62%	57%
1–19	11	11	11	14	10	13
20+	29	33	18	19	27	31
Panel B: Eating Fruit						
Never, almost never	12%	11%	14%	11%	10%	13%
1–6 times/week	66	65	66	67	66	66
At least once a day	23	23	19	22	24	21
Panel C: Eating Vegetables						
Never, almost never	6%	4%	8%	9%	5%	7%
1–6 times/week	60	59	62	62	58	62
At least once a day	35	37	30	28	38	32
Panel D: Exercising for 30 Minutes or More (per week)						
Never, almost never	29%	28%	32%	30%	35%	23%
1–5 times	57	58	54	58	55	60
6+ times	14	14	14	13	10	18

Source: The 1980s Cohort.

In this chapter we've emphasized health *habits*, not just health, and while it is a bit difficult to show you this fact, the 1980s Cohort's behavior regarding smoking, eating fruits and vegetables, and exercising does reinforce the notion that people develop healthy habits or unhealthy ones. As for those habits, it probably won't surprise you that those who smoked at age 20 are a lot more likely to do so at age 25 as well. More surprising, perhaps, is that those that smoked at age 20 are less likely to report that they eat fruits and vegetables or exercise much. But those who often ate fruits are lots more likely to eat vegetables often as well, and also more likely to exercise a good bit. Now, these patterns are not strong and the health-related behaviors that are reported are certainly not the only ones that influence health, but, yes, one does see in the choices by the 1980s Cohort a clear tendency for those who eat healthy foods such as fruits and vegetables also to engage in more exercise and to be somewhat less likely to smoke.

Earlier in the chapter, I pointed out the fact that schooling level and health are generally found to be linked—those with more schooling

Table 6.6: Percentage in "Fair" or "Poor" Health at Age 25, by Education

Bachelor's Degree?	Population	Whites	Blacks	Hispanics	Females	Males
No	10.1%	9.2%	11.7%	11.6%	11.4%	8.9%
Yes	2.5	2.3	4.4	3.0	2.5	2.5

Source: The 1980s Cohort.

tend to be in better health. Table 6.6 suggests that this connection holds for the 1980s Cohort as well, while table 6.7 suggests that these health-related behaviors like diet and exercise are one of the many factors that help make it so. Table 6.6 shows the percentage of those with and without a BA degree who are in "fair" or "poor" health (the two worst health categories in the survey).

We see for the population overall that while 10.1% of those without a BA are in fair or poor health at age 25, only 2.5% of those with a BA are in those health categories. And that pattern is evident for all the subgroups in the table. While not suggesting that this relationship is purely "causal"—meaning that one is a direct result of the other or that education causes good health—this linkage is typical of what we find in many populations and measured in many different ways: those who have more education tend also to be in better health. We see that's true for this 1980s Cohort. To see if there is reason to think this relationship is causal, we can explore this linkage a bit further by considering those health-related behaviors.

Table 6.7 shows each of the four behaviors we've just discussed—smoking, eating fruits and vegetables, and exercising—by the level of education each person has. The table shows that there is a remarkable difference in the behavior by the level of education. While 38% of those without a high school diploma don't smoke, 74% of those with a BA degree don't smoke. Over half of those without a high school diploma smoke nearly every day, but only 11% of those with a college degree do so.

The pattern is also quite strong when we consider eating fruit: while 20% of those with the least education almost never have a piece of fruit, only 7% of those with a college education don't eat fruit. The pattern isn't quite so strong for eating vegetables, but in this case too there are healthier habits among the more educated. For exercise as well, the more educated are a lot less likely never to

Table 6.7: Unhealthy and Healthy Behaviors, by Education Level

Frequency	Education Level			
	Less than High School Diploma	High School Diploma	Some College	Bachelor's Degree or More
Panel A: Smoking at Age 20 (days/month)				
None	38%	59%	68%	74%
1–20	10	11	11	15
20+	52	30	21	11
Panel B: Eating Fruit				
Never, almost never	20%	13%	9%	7%
1–6 times/week	61	65	68	63
At least once a day	19	22	23	30
Panel C: Eating Vegetables				
Never, almost never	10%	7%	5%	3%
1–6 times/week	58	58	59	55
At least once a day	32	35	35	42
Panel D: Exercising for 30 Minutes or More (per week)				
Never, almost never	41%	33%	31%	20%
1–5 times	41	52	57	67
6+ times	18	15	12	13

Source: The 1980s Cohort.

exercise, but they don't seem to do so daily more often than those with less schooling.

So what do you make of these patterns? A cynic would argue it's all just luck—some people are lucky and get a lot of schooling and have good health and live a charmed life. But there's a much more convincing story here, and it's pretty motivating: those who have more education take up habits that are known to be more healthy—they eat better, they exercise, they avoid cigarettes—and consequently (yes, because of that!) they are in better health at age 25 and probably will be in better health all their lives.

Like everything else discussed throughout this book, there's no guarantee, no certainty about this, but there's a strong relationship, a clear pattern. This is the reality, not a vain hope or a cynical joke: those who get more education behave in ways that are healthier, and so they are in fact in better health. The evidence from the 1980s Cohort confirms that.

Now, that might suggest to you a couple things. It may be motivating about getting more schooling, since this health issue is yet another payoff from schooling, another piece of the "return" on the "investment," beyond the higher earnings and greater ease of finding a job. It may also suggest to you that whatever your own level of schooling, the habits those with more schooling adopt seem to be habits that themselves pay off with better health. So schooling aside, you may want to consider avoiding risky behaviors, like smoking, and adopting those good habits, like eating a healthy diet and exercising. Your choice, as all these issues are.

And, relentlessly, these life choices influence your well-being now and in the future. That too is reality, like it or not. You might want to do more of those things that may not be very exciting but are beneficial. It's your choice—make it be one you'll be pleased you made in the years ahead.

Table 6.8 shows some of the relationships between family background characteristics and measures of health and health habits. We see, once again, a pattern here: the higher a father's education is, the lower are every one of these unhealthy measures or habits. (Are you persuaded by now that education has an impressive payoff over time, including in your children's lifetime?) The same is true, almost as consistently, for the mother's age at her first birth. That's true when we compare growing up in an intact family versus a single-parent family (with divorced families in between). And it is also generally true for poverty status.

So is your health determined just by your family, by the choices your parents made long ago? No, but there is a link. It certainly isn't destiny, but it does seem to have a big influence somehow. We've not shown here why or how, but we have shown across the 18 million men and women in the 1980s Cohort that their family of origin has a close link to their behaviors and choices. We've also shown that those choices have consequences for even more outcomes.

If you study the two patterns in tables 6.7 and 6.8, you'll see that the relationship with healthy behaviors is stronger for the person's own education choices in table 6.7 than for the choices made by their parents, seen in table 6.8. One's own choices matter most, but choices that parents made many years earlier certainly play a role.

Table 6.8: Relationship of Family Background and Measures of Health and Health Habits

	Fair or Poor Health at Age		Obese at Age		Smoking (at least sometimes) at Age	Never or Almost Never		
	20	25	20	25	20	Eat Fruit	Eat Veggies	Exercise
Panel A: Father's Education Level								
< 12 years	10%	13%	18%	30%	45%	14%	8%	36%
12 years	6	8	15	25	42	12	6	30
13–15 years	5	6	13	23	41	11	4	26
16+ years	4	5	9	14	35	8	3	20
Panel B: Mother's Age at First Birth								
< 18	8%	11%	19%	32%	43%	16%	8%	34%
18–19	9	11	17	26	43	13	8	34
20–30	6	7	13	22	41	12	5	28
31+	6	7	13	20	35	10	4	23
Panel C: Family Structure at Age 14								
Family intact	4%	6%	13%	22%	37%	10%	5%	25%
Divorced	8	9	16	25	44	13	6	32
Single parent	9	12	19	31	41	15	8	35
Other	9	10	15	25	46	13	6	31
Panel D: Family Poverty Status When Age 14*								
In poverty	9%	12%	19%	30%	40%	13%	9%	34%
Slightly above poverty	6	9	17	27	43	13	6	29
> two times their poverty level	5	6	11	19	41	11	4	25

*Ratio of family income to family poverty threshold less than 1.0, between 1.0 and 2.0, or above 2.0, respectively.
Source: The 1980s Cohort.

There's no reason not to think that will also be true for your children as well.

GOOD HEALTH

There's a lot of pure chance in how good your health is, and also some definite influence of your genes and family background on your health. So it may seem to you that your health isn't an aspect of your life on which you have much choice. That's not so.

As we've seen, you have the capacity to influence your own health by the habits you establish in your daily living and by the strategies you adopt as the CEO of your personal health-generating efforts. While you can't eliminate all the risks to your health, you can substantially lower their likelihood by the choices you make.

In this chapter we discussed the strong connection between schooling level and health among all types of people, and suggested several reasons for that connection. We also discussed the fact that your health decisions have an impact not only on yourself but on those with whom you live and even on those in your community. So externalities are an important factor in thinking about health.

We also focused on the fact that since there is a lot of uncertainty about your health, however diligent you may be in establishing good health habits, it is prudent to insure yourself against the awful expenses that would arise if you did suffer some debilitating health impairment. And finally insurance is not only critical for your own well-being, but it is also an act of love for your family, since they are also at risk for enormous expense, inconvenience, and anxiety if your health is harmed.

| # Wrapping Up

*Man is condemned to be free. Condemned, because he did
not create himself, yet, in other respects is free; because once
thrown into the world, he is responsible for everything he does.*

JEAN-PAUL SARTRE, "EXISTENTIALISM IS A HUMANISM"

There now. We've discussed the five life decisions you have to confront and brought several important elements into the discussion about each. Now instead of looking back at each of these five big choices one by one, let's briefly step back a bit and consider the bigger picture.

THE 1980S COHORT

The facts about the 18 million people born in 1980–1984, the 1980s Cohort, are a good place to start. Those facts offer a lot of useful information that can help you consider so many of the decisions you'll need to make. There are several insights that we can take away from looking over all those tables that describe the Cohort's choices and how they're doing by their late twenties.

The tables reflect a lot of different decisions these people made about every one of the issues we looked at. They did not act in lockstep. Some got very little schooling while others earned challenging advanced degrees. Some got great jobs and others none at all. Some had sex at a very early age while others reported still being virgins at the last interview. Some are obese, some smoke, and some don't exercise, but others report eating fruit every day and most are in great physical health. Their choices reflect the whole array of possible outcomes.

When you see in one of the tables describing the 1980s Cohort that the percentage of the population who did one thing or another was "only," say, 1%, remember that that's some 180,000 people in that population. For the smallest demographic group in most of the tables, Hispanics, 1% is a little under 40,000, and even that is a lot of folks. So, whatever you decide about most of these big issues, you aren't likely to be outside the range of rather typical adult behavior. That doesn't imply that you should just blow it off and not consider your choice carefully, but it does mean that if you do it your way, not the way all your friends are doing it, you'll find you're not alone. That fact should be reassuring.

Another conclusion to take away from the tables is that they make pretty clear that choices have consequences. We've seen that grades in high school are closely linked to expectations about completing college by age 30 and are linked to actual completion of college (table 2.5): only 6% of those with C's in high school have a college degree (so far) while 28% of those with B's and 68% of those with A's have their college degree. The actions and choices while in high school matter. That malleable putty during those high school years became more inflexible and rigid clay by the time graduation rolled around.

Similarly, we saw that wage rates and annual earnings by age 25 were linked to education level (table 3.4). So, too, are general health status and healthy behaviors (tables 6.6 and 6.7). Thus, education is linked to earnings, to health, and actually to a lot of other life circumstances. We also saw that the age at which one marries is linked to the risk of divorce (table 4.8) and to the number of children by age 20 and age 25 (table 5.5). At every stage along the way, the choices at one age are linked to the outcomes at a later age. Choices have consequences. That's a fact the information on the 1980s Cohort tells us loudly and clearly.

There's another fact that those tables make clear, but it is something that's a lot harder to know what to make of: family background—measured as father's education, family income, family poverty status, family structure, or in several cases mother's age at the birth of her first child—is also pretty closely linked to the choices and outcomes of the 1980s Cohort. That's true for every one of these choices—for schooling level (table 2.6), earnings at age 25 (table 3.5), cohabitation (table 4.11), mother's age at first birth and number of children by age 25 (table 5.6), and health status, obesity, and health behaviors (table 6.8).

Does that imply that we are locked in to the circumstances in which we were raised? Are the capabilities we have and the opportunities we receive so connected to the economic and social conditions of our parents that we actually don't have many real choices to make? No. That's not what those tables tell us. Put more accurately, I think that's not the right way to interpret what those tables show.

What they do show us is that family background has a lot of influence on our opportunities and probably on our capabilities, values, and preferences. But it is far from deterministic—it is not destiny. Some of those in the 1980s Cohort whose father did not have a high school education have graduated from college (look at panel A in table 2.6). And some of those who grew up in poverty are among those with the highest earnings by age 25 (panel C in table 3.5).

Human behavior isn't nearly as predictable as, for example, the movements of the planets in our solar system or the reaction between two chemicals combined at a given temperature and pressure. Many of the patterns shown in the tables describing choices of the 1980s Cohort are strong, indeed, but none is iron-clad. In fact, let's look at those who grew up with *four* different "risk factors": a dad who had less than a high school education, a mom who first gave birth younger than age 18, who were raised by a single parent, *and* living in poverty in 1997. There weren't very many in that circumstance, fortunately, but of those who were, more than 5% had completed a four-year college degree. They made a choice. They had a choice, despite a high-risk family background.

That cuts both ways. We just made the point that it isn't destiny that you will have low income if you grew up in poverty. But nor is it certain that your life will be comfortable just because "your daddy's rich and your mamma's good lookin'," as the dated expression in George Gershwin's "Summertime" puts it. Your family's circumstances influence your own a lot, but there is also plenty of room for your own choices and efforts to have a big impact. There are no guarantees, but few obstacles are insurmountable. A reasonable interpretation of the 1980s Cohort data assures us of that.

MAKING SENSE OF DECISIONS

The decisions we've talked about—your schooling and job, having a partner or having and raising children, and your health habits—all have several things in common. First, they are all about you. These aren't the choices you may also confront about reducing our nation's stockpile of nuclear weapons or the proper tax on carbon emissions or whether your community should promote charter schools. We've focused on decisions that affect you personally, but many of the ideas or concepts we've discussed as we went along can also help you reach a judgment about many other choices you'll face.

Second, these five are all decisions with some pretty important long-term consequences for you and for your loved ones. The thing that makes them so important is just that: they have impact on you for a lot of your lifetime, so the choice you make really matters.

Third, while several of these choices are reversible, there's a pretty high cost involved in changing your mind and undoing what you choose, and a couple of them really can't be undone, so for these five the stakes are pretty high.

Fourth, most of these choices are not made at a single moment, but incrementally, a little at a time. That's comforting. It also implies, however, that they can sneak up on you. Since most of these choices aren't made all at once one fine day, you may think you don't really need to make them. But then you'll discover later that the issue is settled, the choice has been made, like it or not. So it's better, in most cases, to realize you face a decision about that matter—your occupation or your health habits, for example—and to give it some serious thought and come to a real decision that you then act upon.

We learned about several concepts that clarify aspects of the choices we talked about. They are also relevant to many other choices you'll make. When you think about it, these concepts have come up because they offer exceptional insight about a particular choice. So, for example, if you are making decisions about helping a loved one or asking someone to offer you some guidance, you'll want to remember the notion of principal-agency: be sure that the incentives of the *agent* (whether that's you giving the advice or someone who is helping you) aligns with the well-being of the *principal*, not the agent's own interests. Any real value in the help you give or receive hinges on that alignment.

Another example: In chapters 5 and 6 we learned about externalities. Many of your choices involve activities that impose *externalities* on others, and you'll want to keep in mind how attentive (or insensitive) you wish to be to those often-hidden but very real effects of your actions on others. Conversely, externalities imposed on you by the activities of others are a legitimate reason why you have a stake in— and a right to influence—their behavior, just as they do yours.

Since so many of the choices we've considered have long-term consequences, we encountered the issue of your *time preference* again and again. Not all choices have a long-term effect, of course, so you'll not need to consider your time preference when considering those.

There are lots of additional choices that are big, complex, and consequential in addition to the five we've discussed here. It can be a smart thing to try to use some of the concepts described in the preceding chapters to address some of those choices. At some point you may face a decision about buying a house or about moving to a different location because of a job or for a health reason. Those are big and important decisions. Your time preference is likely to be relevant for those. Both have important externalities, they involve your non-employment productive activities and your employment, and both involve some *uncertainty*.

You'll confront decisions about whom to have as close friends and how extensively to work to keep those friendships active and valuable. You'll face lots of choices about expenditures for cars and clothes, trips and charities, about support for political candidates, about how best to save some of your income for your retirement, and on and on. The concepts we've used in considering the five life decisions are also relevant in thinking through these and other choices.

Some of the concepts we've introduced describe you personally, like your *time preference* and *sovereignty*. Others relate to your choices about activities and the products they generate, including your production of *human capital*, your skills and capabilities. Others emphasize aspects of the production itself, like the notions of *complementarity, specialization, scale economies,* and *comparative advantage*. Other concepts focus on your interactions with others, such as *principal-*

agency, externalities, and *public goods*. Still others address elements of the world you live in and the systems that arrange our lives collectively, like the concepts about the role of the *marketplace, opportunity cost*, and *prices, scarcity*, and the realities of *uncertainty* and *inequality*.

Notice the symmetry between the point just made and those four elements of choice that were introduced in chapter 1. There, we said a choice involves your values, preferences, capabilities, and opportunities. The several concepts brought up in the intervening chapters pertain to you personally, to your activities and products, to your interactions with others, and to the reality of the world in which you make your choices and live your life.

Both sets start with you; both stress your sovereignty and then expand outward to encompass your world of family, friends, and others who compete with you in markets, and your communities, and, finally, the fact of scarcity itself and the opportunities and limits, uncertainties and inequalities of life. We're back to you. Your choices determine your actions and behaviors, and they in turn define you— for those around you and for yourself.

We've talked about some pretty important concepts and while you're at the book's end, hopefully you'll take these concepts with you as you confront the many decisions ahead. Maybe you'll want to pick up the book again to remind yourself of one or another of these ideas. There's a glossary below that offers a quick reminder of each of the concepts and there are a few suggested readings that elaborate on them for your future reference.

DEFINING ONESELF THROUGH CHOICES

Look at the quotation as the beginning of this final chapter. The philosopher Jean-Paul Sartre emphasized that "existence precedes essence." By that he meant that before someone is *what* he or she is, one lives, and one exists. "Man does not have a fixed essence that is handed to him ready-made; rather, he makes his own nature out of his freedom and the historical conditions in which he is placed."[1] Sartre was talking about "mankind," but his point applies to you personally as a man or a woman.

Your essence, your self-worth, and your contribution to your family and community depend on the choices you make. You *are*, for sure. But your essence, your essential nature, and your value to yourself, to your loved ones, and to your community depend on what you choose to do, how you choose to live your life. That's why these are life decisions—that's why they matter. Make good ones, and good luck to you.

Appendix: *Teenage America at the Beginning of the New Millennium*

Each year there are about 4 million people born in the United States, so over the five years from 1980 through 1984, there were nearly 20 million people born. More precisely, those five years were a little low on births relative to other years—there were in fact 18,230,000 people born in the United States during that interval. On the first day of the twenty-first century, these people were 15 to 19 years old, so we can think of them as teenage America at the beginning of the new millennium. Throughout the book, they are called the 1980s Cohort.

As we looked at decisions made by the men and women in the 1980s Cohort, often called Millennials, we learned that they came from a wide variety of families, experienced varied childhoods, and had very different opportunities and constraints. Families matter. The choices of the 1980s Cohort were inevitably influenced by those made by their parents before them. That will surely be true in your life experience and that of your children. Your choices matter also.

In this appendix, we'll look just a little deeper into the family circumstances of these 18 million people based on a representative sample of those born in that five-year period who were interviewed annually for several years since 1997. To help us understand the circumstances they were coming from when they made decisions about schooling, jobs, partners, parenting, and their health, we'll look at them in the first year of that survey, 1997, when they were ages 12–16. We'll also learn a little about how extensive the information is that was gathered about them and about some of the challenges in collecting and sifting through it.

To begin, let's consider what seems like a really simple fact but turns out to be otherwise: the racial makeup of these 18 million people. Our government provides lots of information about ourselves in statistical tables, and one of the best sources until very recently has been the *Statistical Abstract of the United States*, published each year by the Census Bureau from 1878 to 2012 (yes, 1878!), but then terminated because of budget limits. Race and ethnicity of the population, by age, is one of the many things you can look up. So, based on monthly reports on vital statistics like birth certificates, we can see what the race of those 18 million people is even before we turn to the survey data on the 1980s Cohort. Table A.1 shows that.

You may be surprised to see that "race" is shown for only those who are white, black, American Indian, and Asian. No Hispanic category! The reason is that technically "Hispanic" isn't a race; it's an ethnicity. The government explains it this way: "Race and Hispanic origin are reported separately on birth certificates. Race categories are consistent with [a government standard definition]. In this table all women (including Hispanic women) are classified only according to their race."

But times and customs change. So when the representative sample used to study this population was initiated in 1997, and the interviewers asked these teenagers (or their parent since they were quite young) what their race was, there was an option for them to identify as "other," as shown in table A.2.

A lot of Hispanics in the sample didn't like reporting themselves as either "white" or "black" and insisted on being "other." The survey did ask a separate question about Hispanic ethnicity, so we can

Table A.1: Population Born 1980–1984, by Race (from birth certificate records)

White	81.1%
Black	15.5
American Indian	0.9
Asian or Pacific Islander	2.5

Source: www.cdc.gov/nchs/data/statab/ natfinal2003.annvol1_01.pdf.

Table A.2: Population Born 1980–1984, by Race

White	73%
Black or African American	16
American Indian	1
Asian or Pacific Islander	2
Other	8

Source: The 1980s Cohort.

sort this out, but the confusion that surrounds the notion of "race" or "ethnicity" is typical of the many issues that arise when we study populations and their behaviors.

In every chapter and in this appendix, where we show the facts from the sample that accurately reflects the whole population of 18 million all together, we also show the facts separately for "Whites," "Blacks," and "Hispanics." The whole population will include some groups, like Asians, that are not shown separately in the White-Black-Hispanic part of each table. For the record, for technical sampling reasons, not all these groups are sampled with equal probability. Crucially, however, we know what the probability is for everyone in the sample. The proportion of the whole sample that is "White" is 52%, "Black" is 26%, and "Hispanic" is 21% (and there's a small percentage of 0.9% of mixed race/ethnicity). Those are not the proportions in the whole population born in 1980–1984, where 71% are white, 15% are black, and 13% are Hispanic. So we'll "weight" the data so the numbers we show accurately reflect the whole 18 million population, or the whole "White" or "Black" or "Hispanic" populations.

With that little bit of complexity behind us, let's begin by looking where these people lived in 1997 in table A.3. They were pretty spread out by region of the country, with 19% living in the Northeast, and the largest portion, 34%, living in the South, given the way the regions are defined by the Census Bureau. When we look by race/ethnic group separately, we notice that the biggest difference is that some 61% of blacks live in the South, and as many as 45% of Hispanics live in the West. Not a big surprise, but it is important to re-

Table A.3: Location of Residence, Census Region

Region	Population	Whites	Blacks	Hispanics
Northeast	19%	20%	14%	16%
North Central	26	30	18	11
South	34	30	61	28
West	21	19	7	45

Note: Northeast includes CT, ME, MA, NH, NJ, NY, PA, RI, and VT; North Central includes IL, IN, IA, KS, MI, MN, MO, ND, NE, OH, SD, and WI; South includes all the southern states and the District of Columbia; and West includes AK, AZ, CA, CO, HI, ID, MT, NV, NM, OR, UT, WA, and WY.
Source: The 1980s Cohort.

Table A.4: Location of Residence

	Population	Whites	Blacks	Hispanics
Panel A: Rural and Urban				
Urban	73%	68%	81%	90%
Rural	27	32	19	10
Panel B: Metropolitan Statistical Areas				
Central city	27%	21%	48%	40%
Suburb	53	56	35	55
Not metro	19	23	16	6

Source: The 1980s Cohort.

member that the groups are not evenly distributed geographically throughout the whole United States when we look at some of the choices they made.

When we consider where they live by size of town, there are a couple ways to look at it, either by a rural-urban distinction without worrying about the size of the city, or by a more detailed category that tells us if they live in the inner city or the suburbs. Both are rather interesting, so table A.4 shows both.

Less than one-third of Americans in this age group live in rural areas, and a much larger proportion of whites do so than either blacks or Hispanics. Very few Hispanics (only 6%) live outside metropolitan areas. Blacks live disproportionately in the central cities (48%), while more whites live in the suburbs (56%).

Let's look at the parents of the men and women in the 1980s Cohort whose lives have been followed. A couple important questions for us, and for most others who study this population, are "What was their family background?" and "How influential has it been as a factor explaining the behaviors we observe?" Knowing about their parents and the social and economic circumstances in which they grew up is an important first step, and this is shown in table A.5. Overall, nearly 90% of their mothers were born in the United States. That percentage is far lower for Hispanics, with only 54% of them having a mother who was born in the United States. In this characteristic, blacks and whites are very similar to one another, while Hispanics have more recently immigrated to the United States.

Another characteristic of interest is the age of the mother as her

Table A.5: Mother Born in the United States?

	Population	Whites	Blacks	Hispanics
Yes	89%	94%	94%	54%
No	11	6	6	46

Source: The 1980s Cohort.

Table A.6: Mother's Age at First Childbirth and at the Birth of the Child Born 1980–1984

	Population	Whites	Blacks	Hispanics
Panel A: Mother's Age at Her Firstborn's Birth				
< 20	22%	18%	35%	29%
20–24	44	43	46	44
25–29	24	28	13	19
30–34	8	9	5	6
35–39	2	2	1	2
40 or older	0	0	0	0
Panel B: Mother's Age at the Birth of the Child Born 1980–1984				
< 20	11%	9%	18%	13%
20–24	30	28	34	32
25–29	37	39	32	35
30–34	17	19	11	14
35–39	5	5	4	5
40 or older	1	1	1	1

Source: The 1980s Cohort.

child grew up, and there are a couple facts we might like to know: her age when she first had a child, and her age when she had the child born in these five years of 1980–1984. Table A.6 tells us both of these.

About one in five of these mothers (22%) began their childbearing as a teenager, but a much larger percentage of the black mothers did so—some 35%. A very large proportion of these mothers had begun their childbearing before their thirtieth birthday: 94% of black mothers, 92% of Hispanic mothers, and 89% of white mothers. In more recent decades, a much larger proportion of women have waited until after they turned 30 years old to begin having children, but remember the facts here reflect the behavior of women from the 1960s to the mid-1980s.

The mother's age at the birth of the child we are interested in—the one born in the 1980–1984 interval—is older, but even here, less than one-quarter of the children had a mother over 30 when that child was born.

The marital history of the parents and the structure of the family when the child was first surveyed is another fact that we may wish to consider. Table A.7 shows the marital history of the mothers. We see that a vast majority were, or had once been, married. Notice the large difference in the experience of the black children and the white children in this regard: while only 2% of the white children had a never-married mother, some 24% of the black children did so.

Family structure gets pretty complicated when one tries to list all the various possibilities. These are condensed to a few categories in table A.8. There we see that, overall, more than half of all these 12- to 16-year-old children lived in an intact family in 1997, but, again, among blacks, the percentages are much lower.

Another indicator of the living arrangements of these children is the size of their household. A small percentage of them lived in a household with only one other person, their adult caregiver. It may be surprising to see that a much larger percentage (18% overall and as many as 29% of Hispanic children) lived in a household with more

Table A.7: Mother's Marital History by the Time the Child Was Age 12–16 (1997)

	Population	Whites	Blacks	Hispanics
Ever Married	94%	98%	76%	91%
Never Married	6	2	24	9

Source: The 1980s Cohort.

Table A.8: Family Structure at the Time the Child Was Age 12–16 (1997)

	Population	Whites	Blacks	Hispanics
Intact family	52%	58%	22%	51%
Divorced and remarried	8	10	5	6
Divorced	12	12	13	12
Single mother	9	4	28	13
Single mother, later married	8	6	16	9
Living at times with each parent	8	8	7	6
Adopted	1	1	1	0
All other	3	1	9	3

Source: The 1980s Cohort.

Table A.9: Household Size When the Child Was Age 12–16 (1997)

	Population	Whites	Blacks	Hispanics
Panel A: Household Size				
2	5%	5%	8%	4%
3	18	19	21	14
4	34	37	27	27
5	25	26	20	26
6–9	17	13	21	28
10+	1	1	2	1
Panel B: Number of Household Members under Age 18				
1	24%	25%	24%	19%
2	39	41	33	36
3	23	23	20	24
4	9	7	14	12
5+	5	3	10	9

Source: The 1980s Cohort.

than five people. Table A.9 also shows the number of children under age 18 living in these households, and here too there are large differences by race/ethnicity. There are quite different childhood experiences reflected in these tables.

The highest grade of schooling completed by the mother and by the father is another salient fact that can help us understand some of the choices made by their sons and daughters, as shown in table A.10. (In the cases in which the person has a different biological father and residential father, table A.10 shows the highest grade completed by either of the two, and similarly for their mothers.)

Several things are worthy of note about these educational distributions. Overall, 5% or 6% of these parents did not attend schooling beyond the eighth grade. Notice that a much larger proportion of Hispanic parents had an eighth-grade education or less. This reflects the fact we saw in table A.5 that a large portion of these parents immigrated to the United States, so many didn't actually grow up in a U.S. community and so probably didn't have the access to public education afforded children in the United States.

Twenty-one percent of the mothers and 26% of the fathers completed four years of college and beyond. Here too there are big dif-

Table A.10: Mother and Father's Highest Grade of Schooling Completed

	Population	Whites	Blacks	Hispanics
Panel A: Mother's Highest Grade Completed				
8th grade or less	5%	2%	3%	26%
9th grade	3	2	3	6
10th grade	4	4	6	6
11th grade	5	4	12	6
12th grade	36	36	42	29
13 (1 year college)	8	9	8	6
14 (2 years college)	13	14	12	9
15 (3 years college)	3	3	3	2
16 (4 years college)	13	15	8	6
17	2	3	1	1
18	4	4	1	1
19	1	1	0	0
20+	1	2	0	1
Panel B: Father's Highest Grade Completed				
8th grade or less	6%	3%	4%	28%
9th grade	3	2	3	5
10th grade	4	4	5	5
11th grade	5	5	8	5
12th grade	37	35	51	28
13 (1 year college)	6	6	5	5
14 (2 years college)	12	13	10	9
15 (3 years college)	3	3	2	2
16 (4 years college)	14	16	8	8
17	2	3	0	1
18	5	6	2	2
19	2	2	0	1
20+	3	4	1	1

Source: The 1980s Cohort.

ferences by race/ethnicity. "Highest grade completed" isn't the same thing as earning a degree, so we can't say from this table what percentage of each group had a high school diploma or a college degree.

The economic circumstances of the families in which these young men and women lived were also an important factor affecting the choices they made. Tables A.11 and A.12 show us something of this, their annual income and financial net wealth, and whether or not the family was "in poverty." To set the stage or help in interpreting these tables, it is useful to point out that the government statistics

Table A.11: Family Income and Net Wealth When the Child Was Age 12–16 (1997)

	Population	Whites	Blacks	Hispanics
Panel A: Family Income				
< $5,000	4%	2%	11%	10%
$5,000–10,000	5	3	12	9
$10,000–20,000	11	8	20	20
$20,000–30,000	12	11	15	14
$30,000–50,000	25	27	23	23
$50,000–100,000	33	38	16	22
$100,000–200,000	7	8	3	2
> $200,000	3	3	0	1
Panel B: Family Financial Net Wealth				
Negative (in debt)	6%	5%	9%	7%
$0–5,000	13	7	26	28
$5,000–10,000	6	5	10	9
$10,000–20,000	8	7	12	11
$20,000–30,000	7	6	9	6
$30,000–50,000	9	9	11	9
$50,000–100,000	17	18	13	14
$100,000–200,000	16	20	6	9
$200,000–500,000	13	17	3	5
$500,000–1 million	2	3	0	1
> $1 million	3	3	0	1

Source: The 1980s Cohort.

for the year in question (the most recently completed year at the time of the 1997 survey), shows the U.S. overall median household income to be $35,172. For married couples with children, it was $51,950, while for female householders with children and no spouse it was $18,000. The median income for other household or family types that year ranged from a high near $60,000 to a low near $11,000.[1] The families in which the children born in the years 1980–1984 lived were of many of these types and their family's income is shown in table A.11.

Overall, some 9% of the children lived in families with an annual income under $10,000, and that percentage was as high as 23% for blacks, 19% for Hispanics, and 5% for whites. At the other end of the spectrum, some 10% of all these children lived in families with income in excess of $100,000, and that percentage was 11% for whites, 3% for blacks, and 3% for Hispanics. Clearly, the economic circumstances of these children varied greatly.

Table A.12: Family Poverty Status When the Child Was Age 12–16 (1997)

	Population	Whites	Blacks	Hispanics
Panel A: Family in Poverty?				
Yes	24%	15%	46%	49%
No	76	85	54	51
Panel B: Family's Income-to-"Needs" Ratio				
No reported income*	2%	1%	3%	5%
0–½*	8	4	19	16
½–1*	14	9	24	28
1–2	28	28	29	28
2–5	42	49	23	22
5–10	5	6	2	2
> 10	1	1	0	0

*These three categories, combined, are those "in poverty."
Source: The 1980s Cohort.

We see the same fact when we look at the family's financial net wealth in 1997 (that's a rough estimate of the value of all the family's assets minus all its debts). The median net wealth was about $50,000 but almost 20% (more precisely 19%) of the families had a net wealth of under $5,000 while another almost 20% (more precisely 18%) had a net wealth of over $200,000. About 3% had net wealth of more than $1 million at that time.

The discrepancy in net wealth among the three race/ethnic groups is stark. While 12% of whites had wealth under $5,000, some 35% of blacks and 35% of Hispanics did so. At the upper end of the distribution, 23% of whites had wealth in excess of $200,000, while only 3% of blacks and 7% of Hispanics did so.

When we consider poverty, we see the same race/ethnic disparity. Overall 24% of these children lived in families considered economically impoverished, and by race/ethnicity, the figure is 15% of whites, 46% of blacks, and 49% of Hispanics. Panel B of table A.12 provides more detail. Overall, of the 24% in poverty, some 14% of that total had an income level that is more than half as high as their poverty cutoff, 8% have income lower than half that cutoff but positive, and some 2% had no reported income at all. (The poverty-level cutoff is the level of income below which a family is considered "in poverty" and above which it is considered "not in poverty." That level takes account of the number of adults and children in the family. For the relevant year, 1996, for these families the median poverty cutoff was $16,563, but it ranged as low as about $11,000 for very small families and as high as $22,000 for a few, very large families.[2]) Panel B shows that detail for the three race/ethnic groups. At the higher-income end, panel B indicates that overall some 6% of the children live in families whose income was more than five times higher than its poverty cutoff; that figure was 7% for whites, 2% for blacks, and 2% for Hispanics.

A final parental attribute documented here is the religion of the parents. Table A.13 shows the religion in which the mother was raised and her current religious preference. Table A.14 shows the frequency of her attendance at worship services in the year prior to the interview in 1997.

The vast majority of these parents were raised in a Christian faith, for the population overall and for each of the three race/ethnic groups.

Table A.13: Family's (Mother's) Religious Affiliation

	Population	Whites	Blacks	Hispanics
Panel A: Mother's Religious Affiliation in Which She Was Raised				
Catholic	33%	30%	8%	78%
Protestant I*	24	30	11	8
Protestant II**	37	32	78	13
Jewish	1	2	0	0
Muslim	1	1	1	0
Eastern	0	1	0	0
Other	1	1	0	0
None	3	3	2	1
Panel B: Mother's Current Religious Affiliation (1997)				
Catholic	27%	25%	5%	63%
Protestant I*	21	25	10	6
Protestant II**	41	36	79	25
Jewish	1	2	0	0
Muslim	1	1	1	0
Eastern	0	0	0	0
Other	1	1	0	1
None	8	10	5	6

*Type I Protestants include Methodists, Lutherans, Presbyterians, Episcopalians, and United Church of Christ.
**Type II Protestants include Baptists, Pentecostals, Churches of Christ, Assemblies of God.
Source: The 1980s Cohort.

Table A.14: Frequency of Attendance at Worship Services, in Prior Year (1997)

	Population	Whites	Blacks	Hispanics
None	17%	19%	10%	13%
Less than once a month	26	27	20	25
Less than weekly	21	20	26	25
Weekly	25	25	26	27
More than once a week	11	9	19	10

Source: The 1980s Cohort.

The denomination differed dramatically by race/ethnic group with a large proportion of blacks raised Baptist (Protestant II) and an equally large proportion of Hispanics raised Roman Catholic, while whites are evenly divided among the three Christian denominations. Regarding their current religious affiliation, there is a somewhat larger proportion that reports "none," but a large majority continued to report themselves Christians.

Religious attendance varies also, with more than one in ten (11%) attending services more than once a week and another nearly two in ten (17%) not attending at all. For blacks, there is a substantially larger proportion who attended services more than once a week. Blacks also have the smallest proportion that report never attending services within the past year.

Glossary of Terms

comparative advantage: One has a comparative advantage in producing something if he or she can do so at a lower cost than someone else. This is tricky because it doesn't mean she can produce it faster or better. Yet everyone has a comparative advantage at producing something! The key to understanding this really important but slippery concept is to realize that a person who is very good at one or a few things has a pretty high *opportunity cost* of doing anything else. That is, to do her second-best thing means she is forgoing doing her very best thing and the cost in terms of forgone product is high. Someone who is not so good at other things can, therefore, do this task at a lower cost in terms of what's forgone by his doing it than one who is absolutely better at it. So society, and she and he, are better off if she does what she's best at and he does what he's best at, even if she is actually better at his task than he is! That's the beauty of everyone having a comparative advantage. (For a helpful example of comparative advantage, see page 49.)

complementarity: In producing something, when an increase in one of the inputs makes another input more productive, the two are called "complements." An example would be a machine that makes a worker more productive per hour of work. The opposite of complementarity is "substitutability," and that, as you might guess, is what two inputs are to one another if an increase in one makes the other less productive. An example would be bringing solar energy into a plant that has all the coal energy it needs—maybe you'd like to switch from one to the other, but the two are substitutes, and having more of one doesn't make the other more productive, rather the contrary. These notions also apply to "productive" activities in which you and your partner engage. Examples of substitutability might be when your partner joins you when you are trying to do your taxes—your productivity can decline. Partners can be complements in some activities and substitutes in others: examples of complementarity arise in jointly raising your children, in having a conversation about the movie you both just enjoyed, in making love; examples of substitutability arise when you or your partner is managing your social calendar or doing the dishes or cutting the lawn and the other joins in but really just gets in the way.

consumer sovereignty: In general, the word "sovereignty" means the independent authority and the right to make decisions. Typically the word is used in the context of a nation that has the right to decide and act for itself. "Consumer sovereignty" means the same thing for an individual or a household—the right and the ability to make independent decisions and act on them by buying what it wants in the marketplace. That right and ability is one of the most precious of your assets. You'll want to protect it, insist on it if necessary, and use it wisely on behalf of what you hold dear.

cost and price: Cost is what is given up, used up, or forgone in creating the product. It is the value of all those things used to make that product—the raw materials, people's efforts and time, machines, land, you name it. Typically cost is expressed in money terms, in dollars, for example. Price is the dollar value of what the owner of a product will accept in exchange for it. Price is what you pay for it, while cost is the value of the resources used to create it. Lots of times and for lots of products, the cost is equal to the price, but not always. Sometimes the price is higher than the cost—as when an owner can insist on charging more than it cost, for example, when the owner has a monopoly on that product. Sometimes the price is lower than the cost—as when someone wants to encourage its purchase and is willing to pay part of the cost himself. For example, our government wants to promote public elementary schooling, so it pays much of the cost of elementary schooling and the price to the child's family is well below the cost of providing it. When the market in which you buy the product is competitive and anyone who wants to can offer the product for sale, the price and the cost are more likely to be equal.

economies of scale: A scale economy is the phenomenon that arises in producing something when the cost for each unit is lower if the total amount produced is larger. One of the key reasons for scale economies is fixed costs. You can find economies of scale all over the place—from driving more than one kid to soccer practice, to sharing an apartment with a roommate.

externalities: An externality is an impact of one person's action on another person, but that doesn't include kicking him or kissing him. An externality is more subtle than that: it is typically an inadvertent impact, not an intentional one. It is an externality only if the impact occurs as an unintended by-product (that's not to say it's unexpected). There are probably as many good ones as bad ones, and they are all over the place. The typical example is that my driving a car emits carbon dioxide that fouls the air for you and for me. I have imposed a "negative externality" on you. So does the added congestion on the streets when I drive. You do the same for me if you drive, of course. There are lots of externalities, indeed. Your cheery personality impacts me as well, and that's a "positive externality," so I hope you continue to share it with me. And, really, that's the point: I'd like it if you emitted more of those positive externalities and fewer of the negative ones. There are ways to encourage the one and discourage the other, like requiring a payment from a person generating a negative externality, or rewarding a person generating a positive one.

human capital: A company's capital are the assets it has that are used to produce its products: it's the machinery, buildings, land, reputation, know-how, and so forth. Often the capital is expressed in terms of the dollar value of all those productive assets. Human capital is the same notion but applied to all the assets in a human being: the skills and knowledge, stamina, personality, appearance, location, intelligence, everything that is productive about that person. People invest in human capital, paying in dollars and time and effort to acquire those skills and other personal attributes. Human capital is notoriously "illiquid": it cannot be sold off, unlike the machinery or land that constitutes the capital used by a company. However, like a machine that rusts or a perishable resource left idle for too long, human capital can deteriorate through non-use or depreciate through time, and some of it can become obsolete. Human capital can, however, acquire greater value through use (practice) and relevant experience.

inequality, economic: Unequal just means different, but by economic inequality we typically refer to the fact that the level of income, earnings, or wealth differs among people. "Economic mobility" is the phenomenon of moving from one level of income or wealth to another over time or across generations.

marketplace: The marketplace is a conceptual thing, not necessarily a particular spot. It is anywhere where something is bought, sold, or traded. There are well-organized and highly regulated markets, like the stock market. There are pleasantly chaotic markets like the local flea market. But there is also the notion of a place where people look for jobs and firms look for employees—the labor market. When you are in "the market" for a partner, the local bar, a friend's party, the school cafeteria, or wherever else you might find the person you're looking for can be thought of as the marketplace.

opportunity cost: An opportunity cost is a cost just like any other—the value of what you give up to get some product or service or output. Generally, the transparent money cost of the item isn't called an opportunity cost, while the more hidden cost, one you might not have thought of when listing all the costs, is called an opportunity cost, because it reflects opportunities forgone when you use that resource to acquire the product. The value of the time it takes to get the product is a typical opportunity cost. For example, suppose you go to the store and buy your groceries—what did they cost? They cost what the receipt says, which is the sum of the prices you paid for all the things you bought plus the associated taxes. The opportunity cost is the value of your half hour going to and from the store and standing in line to check out. If you could have seen 30 minutes of your favorite TV show instead and that is worth $10 to you (and is the single best alternative use you had for that half hour you spent at the grocery store), then the opportunity cost of your time was $10. So the groceries actually cost you what the receipt says plus the $10 opportunity cost of your time. Sometimes the opportunity cost of your time is greater than the actual dollar cost, as, for instance, when you buy a $15 book and spend several hours reading it. Notice that the opportunity cost is the value of the one best alternative use of the resource, not the sum of all the many things that resource could have been used for. You can only use your dollar for one thing, and you can only use your hour for one thing. The opportunity cost of your time in any activity is its highest valued alternative use.

principal-agent: A principal-agency relationship is one in which one person (the agent) acts on behalf of the other (the principal). There's really no clear line of distinction between this relationship and one in which you hire someone to do something for you, like give you advice about how to invest or fix your car. The agent takes actions that are intended to benefit the principal—at least that's the idea. Often, however, the agent may have a different agenda and can do things that are of greater benefit to her than to her principal. That's often true of the CEO of a company who acts as the agent for the stock shareholders. It can be true of someone you hire to offer advice, as maybe your physician who gives you advice that may be of benefit to you but more surely benefits his medical practice (in the form of your payment for the service). A keyword when a principal-agency relationship arises is "alignment." You would like the incentives that motivate the agent to be "aligned" with the interests of the principal. That's not always easy to achieve. The notion arises in this book because a parent is clearly the agent for his or her children. It is an important idea, one that you may want to think about anytime someone offers to act on your behalf or give you advice.

production: Production is the activity of converting one set of things into another. Taking some rawhide, thread, needle, human effort, and know-how and converting those "inputs" of material, tools, and labor into a shoe is an example of production. A "production function" describes the process or reflects the recipe that is used to convert those inputs into some output. Manufacturing firms produce the cars, skillets, and shoes they sell. Service firms like banks and schools produce their wares in the same way, converting labor by the tellers and accountants, or the teachers and custodians, into the service products we consume. Families also produce the things they consume. The members of the family produce the dinners they eat, the clean clothes they wear, the nurturance and guidance they extend to their relatives, and the sense of well-being and comfort they provide one another.

public goods: Two attributes define a public good: non-rivalrous and non-excludable. Non-rivalrous means there's no rivalry between us in our use of these goods—that a good can be used by you and me and others all at the same time, and my use of it doesn't reduce its availability to you, and vice versa. Examples? There are more than you might think: the beauty of the Grand Canyon or bright moon on a crisp, clear night. But closer to home, the streetlights in the neighborhood or the absence of potholes in that street are also public goods. I use or consume these things, you use them too, and each of us doing so doesn't diminish their availability to others. The other attribute, non-excludable, means that I can't prevent you from using the item, at least not without incurring cost. If my street has good lighting at night, that's available to you too, whether I like it or not. National defense is a quintessential public good: the country's efforts to protect you from foreign attack is just as available to me as to you, and each of us using it doesn't diminish its availability to the other person, and neither of us can easily prevent someone else from enjoying the benefits of the good. So it's a public good. One of the interesting things about a public good is that the amount of it I have can't be uncoupled from the amount of it you have. So this isn't a good that the marketplace can conveniently determine how much to produce or what its price should be—we have to decide collectively, not individually as we can for most goods we buy. The marketplace just doesn't work well for a public good. The concept comes up in this book because there are lots of public goods within the context of the home, ones that are available to all members of the family. They contribute to the *economies of scale* within the family. They necessitate a collective decision within the family about how much to have, since everyone in the family has equal access to them. It also comes up in thinking about your health, since information about what's healthy to consume or wise to avoid is also a public good. That's true of information generally.

sample: In common usage this means a little subset of the whole thing— "You may like this cake—I'll give you a little sample." In the science of statistics, however, there are some rigorous conditions that, when met, can allow us to use a smaller group from the whole group to know lots about the whole quite accurately. A properly constructed sample is actually hard to get, and too often one hears about a sample that doesn't meet those rigorous conditions, so the small group doesn't accurately tell much about the whole group. The sample that is the basis of the 1980s Cohort information used in this book is, in fact, a proper scientifically drawn sample of the population born in the five years 1980–1984 and living in the United States in 1997. So the NLSY97 sample can tell us much about that whole population of 18 million people.

scarcity: Scarcity is just an inadequate amount of something. It has meaning in the context of acquiring most anything. One can have a scarcity of patience, time, knowledge, opportunity, money, or most anything. The fact of scarcity necessitates choice—if something weren't scarce, one wouldn't need to make a choice. She could have all she wants of that commodity or experience or pleasure. Since scarcity is so common for all of us and in so many ways, there is a science that studies scarcity, and the products of its insights are the ideas that guide the discussion in this book. It's called economic science.

specialization in production: Specialization is attractive because you get better at a task when you do it over and over. There's a close linkage between the ideas of specialization in production and economies of scale in production: the larger the scale, the greater the opportunity for each worker to specialize and get better at doing some tasks since he needn't also do other tasks. Why all this matters for you is that you "produce" a lot of things as you go through your day—usually starting with breakfast—and having a sense of some of these principles of production in the home and on the job can make you more efficient and thereby save you some resources.

time preference: The concept of time preference reflects the fact that humans generally prefer to have or experience something good now rather than later. Ask yourself this: if I offered you a $20 bill and told you that you could have it now or I will give it to you in a week, which would you prefer? Almost everyone would prefer now, not later. There are lots of good reasons for this: if you have it now you will be able to use it during this next week if the need arises; you may be gone next week; I may be gone by next week or might change my mind, so it's risky to wait, et cetera. Now is preferred. The concept gets a bit trickier when we ask by how much you prefer the present over the future: If I offered you a $20 bill now or a $100 bill in a week, you would probably choose to wait for the bigger payment next week (unless I was particularly shady or you knew I was leaving the country this weekend). The amount extra it would take to persuade you to wait a while to get your money is one common way we can measure your time preference—the more it would take to persuade you to wait awhile, the stronger your time preference for the present.

uncertainty and risk: Often used interchangeably, the idea of risk or uncertainty just reflects the fact that you don't know what an outcome will be. That may be because you can't check out a product completely: How safe are those tires? How good is that advice? Will this match light? But it may be because you don't know what else is likely to interfere with your enjoyment from the choice you made: It may rain the day of your big outdoor party. You may become ill and unable to take that expensive airplane trip. Sometimes people use *uncertainty* to describe a situation, like a dangerous hike in the mountains, and use *risk* to describe the possible outcome, like a broken leg. Another distinction is made between a risk when outcomes involve unclear information but that can have measured probabilities assigned to them—like the statistical risk of a car accident per mile driven, and inherently *uncertain* circumstances that cannot have measured probabilities assigned, like life after death.

Sources of Information

For authoritative and accurate, if not always really current, information on most of the things discussed in this book (and more), there's no better source than the U.S. government. For many topics, you can find what you want in the *Statistical Abstract of the United States*, published annually from 1878 to 2012. Unfortunately, our government stopped producing this useful compendium because of budget cuts. Now you will need to go to specific federal agencies and departments to get much the same information (see www.factfinder.census.gov/).

For detailed information, you can go to the relevant agency of the U.S. government. In most of these cases, there is not only excellent general information with more detail than you'll probably want, there's also the opportunity to just type in the search box the topic you're after, and the website will help guide you to the information. Be careful: the Internet has lots of "sources" of information and not all are accurate or honest. You are encouraged to go to the U.S. government agency as your source of most anything it provides data about. You can be confident that the federal government statistics are generally accurate, unbiased, and reasonably complete.

For information about jobs and salaries, employment and earnings, unemployment, inflation, and costs of living, go to the Bureau of Labor Statistics. The BLS is an agency within the U.S. Department of Labor and the source of much economic data used by most organizations (www.bls.gov/).

Demographic data is found at the Bureau of the Census, an agency of the U.S. Department of Commerce. There you'll find all sorts of information about families and living arrangements, marriage and divorce, fertility, ethnicity, immigration, rates of poverty, and a lot of related economic and social data (www.census.gov/).

For information about health, a major source is the National Center for Health Statistics (NCHS), an agency within the Centers for Disease Control and Prevention (CDC) (http://www.cdc.gov/nchs/).

Similarly, for information about education, try the U.S. Department of Education's National Center for Education Statistics, NCES (www.nces.ed.gov/).

The extensive information we have about the men and women born in 1980–1984, whom we have called the 1980s Cohort, is from a data set known as the National Longitudinal Survey of Youth, 1997, or NLSY97. It has been undertaken with oversight and funding by the Bureau of Labor Statistics of the U.S. Department of Labor. The survey has been designed, conducted, and made available to the scientific research community by a collaboration of two organizations: the National Opinion Research Center, NORC, affiliated with the University of Chicago, and the Center for Human Resource Research, CHRR, at Ohio State University. The extensive documentation, description, summary of findings, and availability of these data can be found at www.bls.gov/nls. These data have been the basis of thousands of scientific studies, reports, and monographs. They constitute an important national resource as part of the U.S. federal statistical system. The analysis of this survey information annually yields important new information about the workings of the U.S. labor market and labor force.

And if you're curious about any of the concepts explained in this book, here is a tiny list of some books with very good general information:

Kobliner, Beth. *Get a Financial Life: Personal Finance in Your Twenties and Thirties*. New York: Fireside, a division of Simon & Schuster, 2009.
Mankiw, N. Gregory. *Principles of Microeconomics*. 6th ed. Mason, OH: South-Western Cengage Learning, 2012.
Wheelan, Charles. *Naked Economics: Undressing the Dismal Science*. New York: Norton, 2010.

Notes

CHAPTER TWO

1. Walter Mischel, Ebbe B. Ebbesen, and Antonette Raskoff Zeiss, "Cognitive and Attentional Mechanisms in Delay of Gratification," *Journal of Personality and Social Psychology* 21, no. 2 (1972): 204–18.

2. Walter Mischel, *The Marshmallow Test: Mastering Self-Control* (Boston: Little, Brown, 2014).

CHAPTER THREE

1. If you want to read a delightful account about a group that came close to that idyllic circumstance, look at *The Ohlone Way* about the ten thousand Indians who populated the land from Point Sur to San Francisco Bay some quarter millennium ago. Malcolm Margolin, *The Ohlone Way: Indian Life in the San Francisco–Monterey Bay Area* (Berkeley, CA: Heyday Books, 1978).

2. See David M. Kennedy, *Freedom from Fear: The American People in Depression and War, 1929–1945* (Oxford: Oxford University Press, 1999). The quotation about the "most complex military operation in history" is on page 691; the comment about Eisenhower's smile is attributed to General Omar Bradley, on page 690.

3. Life-expectancy figures from U.S. Census Bureau, *Statistical Abstract of the United States: 2003*. Table HS-16 for the 1900 and 2000 figures. The expectation of life at age 65 is found in table 105 of the 2012 *Statistical Abstract*.

4. Beth Kobliner, *Get a Financial Life: Personal Finance in Your Twenties and Thirties* (New York: Simon & Schuster, 2009), p. 130.

5. U.S. Census Bureau, "Table 2: Earnings by Detailed Occupation: 1999: United States," www.census.gov/hhes/www/income/data/earnings/call2usboth.html.

6. Marianne Bertrand, Claudia Goldin, and Lawrence R. Katz, "Dynamics of the Gender Gap for Young Processionals in the Financial and Corporate Sectors," *American Economic Journal: Applied Economics* 2 (July 2010): 228–55.

CHAPTER FOUR

1. U.S. Census, *Statistical Abstract of the United States: 2012*, table 57.

2. Matthew D. Bramlett and William D. Mosher, "First Marriage Dissolution, Divorce, and Remarriage: United States," *Advance Data from Vital and Health Statistics*, no. 323 (May 31, 2001), fig. 1, p. 6.

3. G. S. Becker, E. M. Landes, and R. T. Michael, "An Economic Analysis of Marital Instability," *Journal of Political Economy* 85, no. 6 (December 1977): 1183.

4. R. T. Michael, J. H. Gagnon, E. O. Laumann, and G. Kolata, *Sex in American: A Definitive Survey* (New York; Little Brown, 1994), p. 46.

5. For a more complete discussion and more evidence about this subject, see E. O. Laumann, J. H. Gagnon, R. T. Michael, and S. Michaels, *The Social Organization of Sexuality* (Chicago: University of Chicago Press, 1994), chap. 11 (by J. Feinleib, W. Dale, and R. Michael), esp. pp. 397–412.
6. The information comes from a sample of men and women in the whole United States in 2009. We can think of these as percentages that apply to the population of adults, not just the roughly 2,500 men and 2,500 women in the sample.
7. Because of the way these data were collected, "marriage" here means a heterosexual marriage, so we can't say anything here about gay and lesbian couples, unfortunately.

CHAPTER FIVE

1. That figure of one in six applies to women born around 1955, but the rate hasn't varied a lot throughout the twentieth century. It was somewhat higher for those born early in the century and lower for those born around 1940. S. E. Kirmeyer and B. E. Hamilton, "Transitions between Childlessness and First Birth: Three Generations of U.S. Women," National Center for Health Statistics, *Vital Health Statistics* 2, no. 153 (2011), fig. 10, p. 11.
2. Centers for Disease Control and Prevention, "National Public Health Action Plan for the Detection, Prevention, and Management of Infertility," June 2014, p. 4. Other estimates suggest a somewhat higher percentage.
3. Ibid., p. 13.
4. Guttmacher Institute, "Fact Sheet: Unintended Pregnancy in the United States," February 19, 2015, http://www.guttmacher.org/pubs/FB-Unintended-Pregancy-US .html. In 2008 the rate per 1,000 women ages 15–44 who are well above poverty (with income more than 200% above their poverty line) was about 23 while for those in poverty their rate was 137.
5. Guttmacher Institute, "Facts on Induced Abortion in the United States," July 2014, http://www.guttmacher.org/pubs/fb_induced_abortion.html.
6. R. T. Michael, "Abortion Decisions in the United States," in *Sex, Love, and Health in America: Private Choices and Public Policies*, ed. E. O. Laumann and R. T. Michael (Chicago: University of Chicago Press, 2001), p. 421.
7. These facts come from a website based on an NPR broadcast: "Facts about Adoption," September 7, 2010, www.pbs.org/pov/offandrunning/adoption_fact_sheet .php.
8. Joyce A. Martin, Brady E. Hamilton, Michelle Osteman, Sally C. Curtin, and T. J. Mathews, "Births: Final Data for 2013," *National Vital Statistics Reports* 64, no. 1 (January 15, 2015), table I-1.
9. U.S. Census Bureau, *Fertility of Women in the United States: 2014*, table 1: "Women's Number of Children Ever Born by Age and Marital Status: June 2014," www.census .gov/hhes/fertility/data/cps/2014.html.
10. Edward P. Lazear and Robert T. Michael, *Allocation of Income within the Household* (Chicago: University of Chicago Press, 1988), p. 138.
11. Mark Lino, *Expenditures on Children by Families, 2013*, U.S. Department of Agriculture, Center for Nutrition Policy and Promotion, Miscellaneous Publication No.

1528-2013, 2014. This publication is available at http://www.cnpp.usda.gov/Publi
cations/CRC/crc2013.pdf.

12. Nancy Folbre, *Valuing Children: Rethinking the Economics of the Family* (Cambridge, MA: Harvard University Press, 2008).

13. If you are interested in looking at those trends over time in the percentage of women (and men) who were in the workforce, one good place to look is Abraham Mosisa and Steven Hipple, "Trends in Labor Force Participation in the United States," *Monthly Labor Review* 129, no. 10 (October 2006): 35–57.

14. J. Peter Nilsson, "Does a Pint a Day Affect Your Child's Pay?: The Effect of Prenatal Alcohol Exposure on Adult Outcomes," IFAU Institute for Labour Market Policy Evaluation, a research institute under the Swedish Ministry of Employment, Uppsala, 2008.

15. National Institute on Alcohol Abuse and Alcoholism, "Fetal Alcohol Spectrum Disorders: Yesterday, Today, and Tomorrow," NIH Research Timelines (Washington, DC: U.S. Dept. of Health and Human Services, October 2010); National Institute on Alcohol Abuse and Alcoholism, "Fetal Alcohol Exposure Fact Sheet," http://pubs .niaaa.nih.gov/publications/FASDFactsheet/FASDfact.html.

16. N. R. Butler, H. Goldstein, and E. M. Ross, "Cigarette Smoking in Pregnancy: Its Influence on Birth Weight and Perinatal Mortality," *British Medical Journal* 2 (1972): 127–30; N. R. Butler and H. Goldstein, "Smoking in Pregnancy and Subsequent Child Development," *British Medical Journal* 4 (1973): 573–75.

17. J. Peter Nilsson, "The Long-Term Effects of Early Childhood Lead Exposure: Evidence from the Phase-Out of Leaded Gasoline," November 2009, Uppsala University and IFAU.

18. There are a couple facts you might like to know showing maternal behaviors by the mother's level of education. The CDC reports the percentage of mothers who smoked cigarettes during their pregnancy in 2008 by their education level. Mothers with no high school diploma: 13.7% smoked; those with a high school diploma: 16.0% smoked; those with some college: 10.3% smoked; and those with a bachelor's degree or more schooling: only 1.3% smoked during the pregnancy. Also from the CDC, the proportion of mothers ages 22–44 who in 2002–2004 breast-fed their babies for three or more months, by their education levels, show those with no high school diploma: 45.8% breast-fed; those with a high school diploma: 43.2% breast-fed; those with some college: 43.7% breast-fed; and those with a bachelor's degree or more schooling: 74.6% breast-fed. Centers for Disease Control and Prevention, "Chartbook: Special Feature: Health, U.S.," 2011, table 8 (smoking), table 27 (breast-feeding), www.cdc.gov/nchs/hus/contents2011.htm#008 and www.cdc .gov/nchs/hus/contents2011.htm#fig27.

19. D. Francis, J. Diorio, D. Liu, and M. J. Meaney, "Nongenomic Transmission across Generations of Maternal Behavior and Stress Responses in the Rat," *Science* 286 (1999): 1155–58; I. C. G. Weaver et al., "Epigenetic Programming by Maternal Behavior," *Nature Neuroscience* 7 (2004): 847–54; G. E. Robinson, "Beyond Nature and Nurture," *Science* 304 (2004): 397–99.

20. Robert T. Michael, "Family Caring and Children's Reading and Math Skills," *Longitudinal and Life Course Studies* 2, no. 3 (2011): 301–18.

21. Pedro Carneiro and James J. Heckman, in *Inequality in America*, ed. James J. Heckman and Alan B. Krueger (Cambridge, MA: MIT Press, 2003), 204.

22. For this and related facts about miscarriage, one good source can be found at www .nlm.nih.gov/medineplus/ency/article/001488.htm. When looking for facts of this nature, the National Institutes of Health, at "nih.gov" is a reliable place to go. The quotation in the text comes from a *MedlinePlus* posting dated November 8, 2012. Another dated October 28, 2014, provides a lot of citations that you can look through that give you additional detail about miscarriages.

CHAPTER SIX

1. Of course, life expectancy is just one of the indicators of health. The evidence is just as strong if we were to look at the relationship of education level and measures of morbidity (that is, incidence of disease) instead of mortality.

2. Probably the best expert on this subject is Professor Michael Grossman at City University in New York. If you want to see some of his thinking about the subject, look at Michael Grossman, "The Relationship between Health and Schooling: A Presidential Address," *Eastern Economic Journal* 34 (2008): 281–92.

3. Centers for Disease Control and Prevention, "Pertussis (Whooping Cough)," February 11, 2013, www.cdc.gov/features/pertussis/.

4. Centers for Disease Control and Prevention, "Smallpox Vaccine Overview," 2009, www.bt.cdc.gov/agent/smallpox/vaccination/vaccine.asp.

5. Bureau of Labor Statistics, "Consumer Expenditures in 2010: Lingering Effects of the Great Recession," *BLS Report 1037* (Washington, DC: U.S. Department of Labor, August 2012), table 1, p. 8.

6. A little primer on measuring BMI: the formula for calculating your BMI is your weight in pounds, divided by the square of your height in inches, all multiplied by the number 703. So, for example, if you are 5 feet 4 inches (64 inches) tall and weigh 140 pounds, that's $[140/(64)^2] \times 703 = 24.03$, so you would be "normal" but getting close to "overweight" since the cutoffs for the four categories are these: BMI less than 18.5 is "underweight"; 18.5–24.9 is "normal"; 25.0–29.9 is "overweight"; and over 30.0 is "obese." You can go on the Internet, of course, and find a BMI calculator that will do the math for you if you want to see your own BMI. We might note as well, that BMI is not the only useful measure of obesity.

CHAPTER SEVEN

1. William Barrett, *Irrational Man: A Study in Existential Philosophy* (Garden City, NY: Doubleday Anchor Books, 1962), 102.

APPENDIX

1. John McNeil, "Changes in Median Household Income: 1969–1996," *Current Population Reports Special Studies* P23-196 (July 1998), table 4.

2. Carolyn J. Hill and Robert T. Michael, "Measuring Poverty in the NLSY97," *Journal of Human Resources* 36, no. 4 (Fall 2001), table 1, p. 734.

Index